G.R.O.W.T.H.S. U.P.®

GENERATING REVENUE WITHOUT THE HASSLE OF SALES WHILST UPLIFTING PERFORMANCE

MR BRUCE P LAWSON

G.R.O.W.T.H.S. U.P.®

Generating Revenue Without The Hassle of Sales whilst Uplifting Performance

The book for all those who hate selling but need to increase customers and revenue

Author Bruce Lawson

BaHons, MPRracNLP, PRAC EFT, GQHP, ADV PRAC EMO, CISD, MISMA

ISBN-10: 1514332477
ISBN-13: 978-1514332474

DEDICATION

GROWTHS UP®

This book is dedicated to my two wonderful daughters Dafna and Galia who are a continual joy and inspiration to me. My pride in them is total and my thanks and love endless.

CONTENTS

PREFACE

Congratulations on deciding to change how you deal with your customers and choosing to ditch that dreaded, stressful and uncomfortable sales process.

In this book I will show you how you can ensure that Your GROWTHS UP without having to resort to sales hype, manipulative selling skills or aggressive techniques.

G.R.O.W.T.H.S. U.P. stands for: Generating Revenue Without The Hassle of Sales whilst Uplifting Performance. In this book you will find a natural method to increase the number of your customers and improve your revenue generation without the stress and upset that a normal "Sales process!" engenders.

This book is for anyone who needs to ensure their G.R.O.W.T.H.S. U.P. but hates the idea of "Selling", "Closing", "Demanding money" or manipulating others. It is also for managers and CEO's who have to motivate non-professional sales people (people whose core job is not selling) to develop new customers and increase revenues. The techniques illustrated here as part of the G.R.O.W.T.H.S. U.P. model, aimed at just these kind of people, will help you manage, inspire and motivate them to success.

If this is you, then please read on and enjoy this stress-free natural journey that will help you to ensure your G.R.O.W.T.H.S. U.P, the gentle, moral, congruent way. You can even feel good while following this process, which offers less hassle and pain, and more smiles and satisfaction.

Sounds right? Then read on, and good luck.

This book will be supported by a website, a video blog offering tips, and coaching workshops that are available in person or via Skype. Please contact me for more details at: email growthsup@gmail.com or

- see my website: www.growthsup.co.uk
- or Facebook page: www.facebook.com/copewellbeingsgrowthsup
- or Twitter @copewellbeing

Bruce Lawson, Kent, October 2015

ACKNOWLEDGMENTS

This book developed out of a series of insights I had over recent years regarding how difficult it was for non-sales people to find a positive, relevant way to increase income and customers without being kept in a straitjacket of old, irrelevant thinking cycles, processes and manipulation. On researching the literature, I found little that was original in addressing this problem. Using my NLP background along with my other therapeutic training, I coupled this to my stress awareness skills and married them to my many years of selling and sales training. The result is this book.

The illustrations are by David Frankum, a great and creative illustrator (a big thank you for all your hard work and amazing imagination). His website: www.daveyf.co.uk/

Much of this book was written in my favourite coffee shop in Faversham – Jittermugs – where the owner Nick played genial host to my typing and musings. Thank you.

To the reader, I hope this book and the model it contains transports you to a prosperous, stress-free, relaxed and positive place.

.

1 INTRODUCTION

Again, congratulations on deciding to change how you deal with your customers and for ditching that dreaded, stressful, uncomfortable sales process.

This book introduces you to the G.R.O.W.T.H.S. U.P. model

G.R.O.W.T.H.S. U.P. stands for: Generating Revenue Without The Hassle of Sales whilst Uplifting Performance. The model replaces old-style aggressive, combative sales processes and sales targets based on revenue and closes with a natural method that will increase the number of your customers and improve your revenue generation, all the while staying relaxed, focused, congruent and motivated.

The book will first outline what G.R.O.W.T.H.S. U.P. is as an overview of the model and introduce you to some of the underlying concepts and trends. We will then go through why you might hate sales and how the model will replace those hates with something positive and substantive with concepts that will motivate and reinforce your well-being and boost your self-image.

After that we will set the scene in how you can get the most out of the model by identifying and then helping you discard some bad habits, old thoughts and old-style thinking that you may have picked up or had foisted on you in the past. This is to clear the way to help you gain the most traction from the G.R.O.W.T.H.S. U.P. model.

To reinforce that clarity, in Section 2, we will begin by helping you develop a PMA (Positive Mental Attitude), which is essential to help you maximise the model. We will offer you tips and techniques to get you feeling positive. We will show you ways to stay there – by reinforcing your self-image, improving your motivation and beginning the process of helping you stay focused, being congruent and in control.

Now that you are in the right frame of mind to optimise use of the model, the rest of this section offers you a series of techniques to obtain the best results. Using easy-to-remember acronyms, we will learn how to S.M.I.L.E. Then you'll learn how to have that natural conversation by having a N.I.C.E.

C.H.A.T. To help you even further we will explore the concept of N.O.I.S.E. and how, by understanding and breaking through it, you can stay relaxed and positive and so generate more revenue and customers.

We will add to this by showing how staying on the right PA.T.H. will help you with your conversations, exchanges and transactions. Finally in this section, we will bring it all together by introducing you to the FCO^2 Formula of Focus, Congruence and Control, which in the G.R.O.W.T.H.S. U.P. model brings maximum return while you stay energised, happy and productive.

In Section 3, we now look at how to apply the G.R.O.W.T.H.S. U.P. model by taking you on a journey of DisCRETioN where, at each station, we will show you how to apply the tools to naturally generate more customers and revenue. We will follow your and the "Customer's path" so you can see through their eyes, and hear through their ears, how they react to you, thus building on the previous chapter's insights.

We will explore different encounters, from face-to-face to telephone; from email to instant messenger; from social networks to Skype. All have different optimal times for use and methods that will maximise the G.R.O.W.T.H.S. U.P. model and enhance your revenue through completed transactions.

By this stage you should be in a positive frame of mind, understand the G.R.O.W.T.H.S. U.P. model and how to apply it for maximum results. Section 4 will be our conclusion where we bring all of what we have discovered together and learn how to extend that natural conversation and the model into the larger and often overlooked, wider space.

Section 5 is where our appendices sit and will include the full list of acronyms and their definitions; some visual models referred to in the book; exercises to help you stay positive, to remove stress and help you sleep better, stay focused, congruent and in control.

Finally a list of contact details and video blogs that can be used as an accompaniment to this book are included. The book will be published as both an e-book on Amazon and will be available as a hard copy.

Please enjoy the rest of this book and your stress-free, relaxed future where your G.R.O.W.T.H.S. U.P.

2 WHAT IS G.R.O.W.T.H.S. U.P.?

G.R.O.W.T.H.S. U.P., is all about Generating Revenue Without The Hassle of Sales whilst Uplifting Performance. This book and its accompanying project is about helping you find a natural method that can increase customer numbers and improve revenue generation without the stress and upset that you feel when you try to sell the old-fashioned, manipulative, scripted way.

The concept grew out of a realisation that most people who are not by profession salespeople, but nevertheless have to sell their product or service, generally hate that part of their business.

If you are a naturally creative person or entrepreneur, the focus of your mind and body and the enjoyment it brings is on the creative side of your product or service. That is where you get the most pleasure and satisfaction. Creating and developing something you believe in, and feeling the joy of that birth and the development of your idea or service, is where you want your focus and energy to be. The selling side is not something you look forward to or enjoy because your mind and soul are elsewhere. If that is you, then this book is for you.

Maybe you're a manager, or someone employed in a business where your primary focus might be caring or looking after others, or making or developing a product or service, or managing that product, service or unit. Unfortunately, due to the structure of the company, the senior management also expect you to sell this product or service. Though this is part of your job, it is the part you hate, avoid and do least well. If this is you, then again G.R.O.W.T.H.S. U.P. is definitely for you.

G.R.O.W.T.H.S. U.P. is a natural method that you can practice and internalise for stress-free results that will bring an increase in happy customers and revenue generation. Because it is natural, there is no resistance from you or your customer. This method is therefore easy to internalise and simple and relaxing to use.

The principles as outlined in this book are no more and no less than to help you unlearn old, painful, unsettling habits of sales techniques and manipulative practices and replace them with a natural relaxed conversation where being focused and in the moment you will be able to naturally gain customers, generate revenue and feel good while doing it. This will give you confidence, reduce stress, and improve your bottom line.

G.R.O.W.T.H.S. U.P. will guide you through a series of natural concepts and techniques that are easy to adopt and simple to use. Once you have practiced them and used them in a relaxed, natural, flowing way, you will find the G.R.O.W.T.H.S. U.P. method will help you feel calm, relaxed and successful without having to resort to stressful unpleasant and uncomfortable, old-style sales techniques.

We will use a series of acronyms to embed these new ideas and natural processes in your mind, making them easier to remember, internalise and use.

These will be backed up by chapters on: applying G.R.O.W.T.H.S. U.P., and using our journey of DisCRETioN. We will examine your natural conversation and its delivery in the physical and digital space. We will look at face-to-face meetings, telephone, Skype, email, social media (including Twitter, Facebook), as well as providing appendices with extra detail and valuable exercises.,

Because you will feel relaxed and comfortable with this approach, you will be less stressed, accomplish more and grow your business, all the while feeling calm – thus helping you concentrate on the areas of your work you enjoy the most. It is a Win-Win.

With G.R.O.W.T.H.S. U.P. you will distance yourself from sales which frighten, stress that makes you feel uncomfortable and which puts you under primary and secondary stress that affects how you work in the parts of your business you do enjoy. Instead you will embrace a relaxed process that you can engage in and feel comfortable with. Rather than avoiding customers and sales – which hinders your business growth – you will be transformed into someone who embraces customers and revenue growth as part of a relaxed, enjoyable process that allows you not only to grow your business but also enjoy the creative side, thus giving you more energy, time and satisfaction.

This is G.R.O.W.T.H.S. U.P.: a natural method to help you grow your business and feel good at the same time.

This book and the project associated with it, which you can find on Facebook and on the website, includes support through workshops and Skype training so you get the most out of G.R.O.W.T.H.S. U.P. Find out more at: www.growthsup.co.uk

Section 1 Setting the scene

3 WHY YOU HATE SELLING

Before we look at how G.R.O.W.T.H.S. U.P. can help you, it is important to review why you and people like you hate the idea of selling and why it stresses so many professional people, entrepreneurs, managers and owners of small- and medium-sized businesses.

Once we have clarified what factors make sales so unattractive to you, we can then show you how G.R.O.W.T.H.S. U.P. addresses all of these concerns and dislikes.

To succeed, all businesses have to grow. To grow you obviously need to increase your revenue, add more customers and obtain the maximum from the customers you have.

Up until now you probably felt that the only way to achieve this was to subject yourself to high-pressure sales techniques or manipulative scripts and rigid sales processes.

The first reason you probably hate selling is that this is not you.

Your main role in your business is to be creative or to manage people or build opportunities and develop your brand. Your head and your heart are not designed for selling, so that when you have to undertake that role it feels like it is going against all that you feel good about in your business. You probably see the sales you have to make as cold, unfeeling manipulative, demanding and aggressive whereas your focus is probably on being creative, caring, having long-term views as well as managing design and creating the opportunities to develop your business.

So the first reason you hate sales, as we will explain in more detail later, is because the sales process as defined by old-style thinking and is incongruent to you. Later, when we reach the chapter on FCO^2 ,you will understand in more detail how important congruence is to you in achieving your goal in a focused, positive, natural and relaxed way.

So you hate sales because it goes against the grain; it makes you feel awkward and incongruent. G.R.O.W.T.H.S. U.P. is a natural, relaxed process which avoids this by focusing you on the power and gentleness of natural conversation; a N.I.C.E. C.H.A.T. as we describe it.

Now that we have set the scene by highlighting the strategic reason you hate sales, let's look at some specific factors that make sales so unpleasant to you. We will start your G.R.O.W.T.H.S. U.P. journey by explaining in brief how G.R.O.W.T.H.S. U.P. avoids or mitigates each of these unpleasant factors.

Let's begin the detailed look at your dislike of sales by examining what I call the RESISTANCE SLB (SELF-LIMITING BELIEF).

In the old sales process you assume the customer is your enemy and will be resistant, and you have to battle to get your sale, which is your objective. You feel combative, aggressive, nervous, and this will reflect how you deal with the customer and how they respond to you. If you do get the sale by manipulative, aggressive techniques you still feel bad as this is not how you like to operate. If you don't get the sale you feel bad because you haven't met your goal or target. Either way it's a Lose-Lose

Contrast this with the G.R.O.W.T.H.S. U.P. model where your goal is just to have a N.I.C.E. C.H.A.T. You see the customer as a friend and a person; your mental state is relaxed and positive and consequently your chat is relaxed and natural. Then if you have found common ground and the customer wants to buy, you have succeeded in your goal and feel good. If the customer does not want to buy your product then you have still succeeded as your goal was to have a NICE CHAT, which you have had; so you still feel good. This is a Win-Win.

The two diagrams below illustrate this different approach.

THE FIRST IS: THE OLD SALES RESISTANCE SLB [SELF-LIMITING BELIEF]

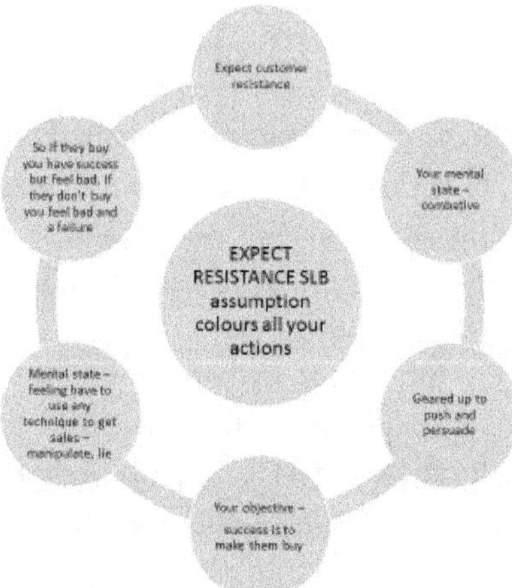

THE SECOND IS: THE G.R.O.W.T.H.S. U.P. MODEL

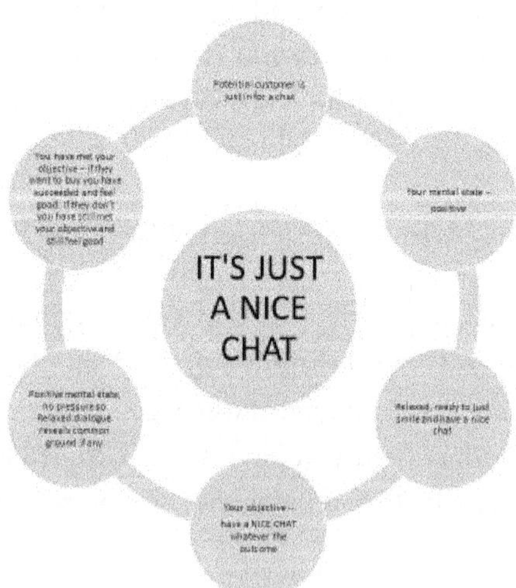

Coupled to this resistance model is, of course, the very common fear of:

REJECTION

In the old sales model, success is predicated on you selling, so if you don't sell and your aggressive technique is rejected by the customer and they don't buy, you take it personally: because your mental state has invested all your energy and emotion in completing the sale.

Be rejected once and it feels bad; your soul weeps. That then makes it much harder to repeat the process and the fear of rejection, and how you feel about it, impedes your actions. If you are rejected several times, and this is more than likely in the old sales process, then you will feel terrible, emotionally drained, without energy, and like a deflated balloon. Each rejection will make it harder and harder for you to try and sell until eventually you will give up.

Not only that, but the emotional state the rejections trigger make it harder for you to be creative and function in the rest of your business; so it is likely your creativity and productivity will also suffer even in those areas of the business you enjoy.

Sound familiar?

Contrast this to the G.R.O.W.T.H.S. U.P. process where rejection is impossible. Your only goal here is to have a N.I.C.E. C.H.A.T. That is easy to achieve, allowing you to be relaxed knowing you will easily and naturally meet your goal. No fear of rejection, so you can enjoy the G.R.O.W.T.H.S. U.P. process; and that will inevitably lead to rejection-free encounters. Such relaxed, natural dialogue will result in more revenue and customers and leave you feeling so good at your success of just having N.I.C.E. C.H.A.T.s that you will be happy to repeat the process, time and time again. This will also improve your mental state allowing you to focus on the creative side of your business in a positive, energised and congruent way. What a contrast.

The next area of sales that worries people is what sales training calls:

QUALIFYING OBJECTIONS

Of course the fundamental flaw in that model and the old sales cycle as shown above is that it presumes a negative from the start. You are trained to expect objections and then have to qualify or counter them.

You are already in a negative frame of mind assuming there will be barriers raised to your sale and so your mental state is aggressive and combative, and this feeds into your customer who will also become the same. You end up in a battle that never needed to exist.

So in the old model, if you are able to qualify the objection it often leads to another because of the negative state you and the customer are in. Even if doesn't, you have succeeded in just one part of the sale process and are still looking out for objections and barriers; so you feel stressed and anxious even if you have succeeded in qualifying that objection. What a hassle for nothing.

Now let's look at in contrast the G.R.O.W.T.H.S. U.P. model.

In this model there are no objections possible as there is nothing to object to. You are having a N.I.C.E. C.H.A.T. with your customer, eliciting information in a natural, relaxed way. You don't have to worry, prepare for, or be stressed out by the inevitable objection because it doesn't exist. You can stay relaxed as your natural conversation will either lead to an interest and an exchange or it won't. As your objective is not to sell but to just chat, then either the customer is interested or not. There is no objection to worry about. The most you will get is a request for clarification, which you can offer or not. So no qualification, no worry, no stress.

With the G.R.O.W.T.H.S. U.P. model you stay relaxed and steer clear of negative behaviour, attitudes and talk; leaving you relaxed and comfortable in both your natural conversations, your N.I.C.E. C.H.A.T.s, and the main focus of your business, undistracted by fear or negative and disruptive emotions.

Another area of concern, and why people hate selling is:

ASKING FOR MONEY

It is certainly not a natural part of the British culture – and in some other cultures – to talk about, discuss or bargain about money. The process leaves most people embarrassed, worried and fearful and therefore is avoided, postponed or handled badly. Worse, as this usually comes at the end of the sales process (which is stressful enough anyway), a lot of us either bottle out or totally mishandle this part of any business exchange.

So by the time you get to ask for the money in the old-style sales process, your mental state is combative, fearful, probably confused and angry, and that reflects on your customer who is in a similar state and is expecting to be ripped off, bamboozled or tricked. This is not a good place to be either for you emotionally or for your business.

Now let's look at the G.R.O.W.T.H.S. U.P. approach.

First, as this is a positive, relaxed, natural process where your objective is not to sell but to just have a N.I.C.E. C.H.A.T., by the time you come to the exchange and then to tie-up the transaction (as you will see in more detail in the chapter on C.H.AT.) both sides are in a relaxed state where the process flows so naturally that the customer wants the goods or service, has committed to it and now wants to pay for it.

Yes that's right. They want to pay for it as it is a natural conclusion to the process. As has often been quoted: 'People love to buy but hate being sold to. 'Well here is the perfect situation: you have sold nothing, just had a natural conversation that has led inevitably to their desire to buy. In this relaxed, safe, secure, emotional environment, asking for money is just a simple conclusion to the G.R.O.W.T.H.S. U.P. process. No stress or fear, just a genuine price that values what the customer wants to buy.

The exchange takes place in an atmosphere of calm good humour. The customer gets the goods or service and you get paid. Painless, easy, natural. It's so easy you are happy to do it again. Another Win-Win.

This area of concern is linked closely to another dreaded part of the old-style sales cycle:

THE CLOSE

Again in the old-style sales cycle, you are geared up to having to "Close" the deal. This can cause anxiety as in this model it is your objective, but you are worried. What if I fail or can't close? I will be seen as a failure; my manager will criticise me; my business will fail. All this pressure causes a negative mental state, makes you nervous, is transmitted to the customer, and the result is often a failure to close, or exhaustion even if you do succeed.

Again even the word "Close" is inappropriate as it suggests the end of something when in fact a successful conclusion should be the start of, or part of, an ongoing relationship. You close, you walk away, you build a relationship and you have ongoing success. That is what the G.R.O.W.T.H.S. U.P. model offers. Let me show you how.

In the G.R.O.W.T.H.S. U.P. model we are not looking to sell or, therefore, close. We are just having a N.I.C.E. C.H.A.T. If that naturally leads to an exchange, then tying up the transaction is a natural outcome of the relationship, which is built in the stress-free, relaxed environment of the N.I.C.E. C.H.A.T. you have just had. It has flowed naturally and both sides want the conclusion of the transaction, which is the exchange of money for goods or services. As this is done in a mutually supportive win-win environment, there is no “Close”. There is a natural fulfilment of the desires of both sides and the foundation for future or ongoing exchanges. No pressure, no stress and a built-in, long-term option.

All of this will be explained in much more detail in the following chapters in which you will see how a S.M.I.L.E. and a N.I.C.E. C.H.A.T. will take you on the P.A.T.H. to a successful stress-free outcome, generating more revenue and an increase in customer numbers.

A word then about another area of selling that you and others hate:

TARGETS

These are usually set by external influencers – such as managers who really aren’t that good at managing and don’t really understand your constraints or concerns – or by yourself where you have been conditioned to believe that certain targets or KPIs (Key Performance Indicators) are essential for the success of your business.

These targets are usually focused on: the number of clients you talk to; the conversion rate; the number of successful closes, and the amount of revenue each close brings in, and so on.

Because you are focusing on aspects that worry and stress you and are not congruent with your main area of business, the targets, instead of being an incentive to improve, becomes an anchor that drags you down. Each time you fail to meet a target you feel more dispirited, more stressed and less likely to add more revenue or customers to your business.

Targets or goals are not wrong for a business or individual. It is just that they have to be the right targets and goals. They have to stimulate, energise and motivate because they are congruent with how you operate; not punitive, detached and imposed upon you.

In the G.R.O.W.T.H.S. U.P. model, as you will see later, your goal is just to have a N.I.C.E. C.H.A.T., with as many people as you feel able, via as many channels of communication you have access to.

As this target is non-threatening, does not interfere with your main business goals and focus, and is easy to achieve, then it is not to be feared but embraced. Each successful chat makes you want to have another one; and this target – rather than impeding and scaring you – actually stimulates and empowers you; leading to more N.I.C.E. C.H.AT.s, more revenue and customers – and you feel good about it at the same time.

We will look at how you apply this target to your business in more detail in later chapters. It is still challenging and will push you but in a congruent, positive way, which will stimulate you to reach success – not penalise you for failure.

Finally in this chapter on what you hate about selling, I want to include the idea of:

SELF-IMAGE

Many people like yourself hate selling because it attacks, threatens and destroys their self-image. The old-style selling model is, for many people, one that leads them to feel a failure; weak, disempowered and deeply unhappy. This directly affects how you and they conduct the rest of their business and can have a serious impact on social relationships.

Businesses and relationships thrive when one has a PMA (Positive Mental Attitude), more of which later. Suffice it to say, when you feel focused, congruent and in control, as I will illustrate in my chapter on FCO^2, your energy and your view of the world is strong, powerful, motivated and positive. This view will help you be successful in your business and happy at home.

The old-style sales process can sap your will and leave you in a negative mental state. The G.R.O.W.T.H.S. U.P. model does the opposite. Here's how.

G.R.O.W.T.H.S. U.P. focuses on you being relaxed and just having a natural conversation – a N.I.C.E. C.H.A.T. G.R.O.W.T.H.S. U.P. takes you down a path of natural, relaxed conversations; of building a meaningful long-term relationship (where relevant) and having a no-pressure conversation.

This means that your self-image is intact and is actually reinforced. You are congruent with yourself, your values, the rest of your business and positive in how you see the world. This means the positive, reinforced self-image that G.R.O.W.T.H.S. U.P. offers, allows you to be strong, motivated and shine in your business and in your personal life.

As we have seen, G.R.O.W.T.H.S. U.P. does this by avoiding: incongruous sales processes, expecting resistance, expecting objections that need to be qualified, demands for money and manipulative practices. There are no fearful closes or punitive targets in the G.R.O.W.T.H.S. U.P. model.

So in this chapter we have looked at some of the reasons why you and many others hate sales and therefore avoid it, and in doing so don't maximise opportunities. We have introduced you to how the G.R.O.W.T.H.S. U.P. model counters all the fears and hate and offers a model that is supportive, positive and natural, leading to Generating Revenue Without The Hassle Of Sales whilst Uplifting Performance.

In the following chapters we will show you how this model works and how you can achieve your G.R.O.W.T.H.S. U.P., while remaining happy, relaxed positive and strong.

I hope you enjoy the journey down this path to success.

4 GETTING RID OF BAD HABITS, OLD THOUGHTS AND OLD-STYLE THINKING

In Neuro-Linguistic Programming (NLP) there is a saying. 'If you always do what you have always done then you always get what you always got.'

In other words, to change your approach and attitude you have to think and do something completely different, not just try and tinker with what is not working.

So it is with G.R.O.W.T.H.S. U.P.

G.R.O.W.T.H.S. U.P. will help remove the hatred of sales and replace it with a natural, relaxed method that will be enjoyable and yield results. You, to use it to its maximum and achieve your goals, need to banish old thoughts and processes that have made you unhappy, frustrated, depressed and stressed and replace them with a completely different view: the G.R.O.W.T.H.S. U.P. view, the G.R.O.W.T.H.S. U.P. PA.T.H. to success, using a relaxed natural flowing model.

It may sound easy but most of us find it hard to abandon old practices we are familiar with however much we hate them. There is comfort in the familiar even if it is a negative familiarity.

So in this chapter we are going to help you remove the old and put on the new; preparing you to fully embrace and use the G.R.O.W.T.H.S. U.P. model for maximum effectiveness and fun and minimum stress.

Some bad habits

- The first one is setting yourself up with: unrealistic targets.

  One bad habit it is easy to be sucked into – either by yourself or by your managers – is to have to perform to unrealistic targets. Targets or goals that stretch and are S.M.A.R.T. [Specific, Measurable, Achievable, Realistic and Time-based] are fine in helping keep you on track as long as the targets are the right ones.

However, if the targets are measuring the wrong effort or are unobtainable, then all that happens is that you are set up for failure and disappointment. Research has shown that targets only work if they are reasonably easy to attain. Make them too difficult and, far from motivating, they demotivate and reduce performance.

Targets in the old-style sales process usually focus on: number of closes, deals done or revenue gained. These can put undue pressure on the person, and in fact reduce not increase their effectiveness. The by-product is a negative mental state that not only affects sales performance, but also performance and productivity in the other areas of the business the person is responsible for.

Often, inexperienced managers, pressured from above, are pushed to perform and pass that pressure on to you in the form of unrealistic targets.

This is a recipe for disaster and should be avoided at all costs. If it is you setting the targets, be kind to yourself and adopt the G.R.O.W.T.H.S. U.P. model and then you will be using a positive method that will reinforce your motivation and performance.

G.R.O.W.T.H.S. U.P. targets are based solely on having a number of N.I.C.E. C.H.A.T.s. The target is to complete the conversation in a positive way. Quality not the quantity is the goal. This ensures your targets motivate and empower, leading you to want to meet and exceed them; keeping you positive, aligned and energised and ensuring all parts of your business prosper.

- Another bad habit it is easy to slip into is what I call an error in timing.

Outside pressure to perform, enthusiasm or ignorance can lead to contacting customers at the wrong time or, if using old-style sales scripts, using the wrong part of the sales cycle at the wrong time, thus damaging the prospect of a sale. Let us look at each of these separately.

Firstly, contacting potential or existing customers (unless they walk in to your place of business) is an area you should consider carefully to ensure your G.R.O.W.T.H.S. U.P. model works best. There are times in the week and the day that emails, telephone contact or instant messenger may not be appropriate, whereas posting a note on social media may be suitable. We will look at this in more detail in the chapter on "Connect" in Section 3 (Applying G.R.O.W.T.H.S. U.P.).

In brief, Monday morning and Friday afternoon are not great for telephone calls or emails. Tuesday at 11 am is best for emails. Calls should be made between 08:00 and 12:00 and 14:00 and 16:30 Tuesday to Thursday.

Facebook and other social media can be posted at any time as people will access it when they want.

Twitter is more immediate, so I would suggest Monday before 08:00, or maybe if you have commuters as customers, after 17:00 and before 19:00 Monday to Thursday.

The second error: this occurs if you are using old-style sales scripts; here, under pressure to perform and distracted, not in the moment, you end up using the wrong part of the sales cycle at the wrong time, thus damaging the prospect of a sale, unlike in the G.R.O.W.T.H.S. U.P. model

By this I mean focusing on qualifying an objection because you are expecting resistance when in fact the customer is giving you a buying signal; or carrying on with your presentation when the customer has signalled they wish to conclude the deal. In sales speak, missing a closing or buying signal.

Has this happened to you? Most reluctant salespeople let the pressure, the script and the process take over so they are not in the moment and miss the signals. This creates tension and frustration in the customer and is likely to result in no sale.

Contrast this with the G.R.O.W.T.H.S. U.P. model where timing is dictated by the natural flow of the conversation. You cannot get into this bad habit or commit this error as the model allows you to have a N.I.C.E. C.H.A.T., and the natural flow of the conversation – as we will see in detail later – takes you to a natural conclusion, which either results in a transaction or a completed conversation with relaxed participants, both of which are a valid exchange.

- The third bad habit people often fall into is: using the wrong approach.

If you are conditioned by and married to the old-style sales cycle and process, the lack of flexibility that this rigid cycle requires and the aggressive, combative attitude it engenders, will lead to error. It can mean that instead of going with the flow, as in the G.R.O.W.T.H.S. U.P. model, you are trapped in a way of communicating with your customer that means you can be out of sync with them, which can lead you to using the wrong approach.

Being assertive when they need clarification; waiting for an objection when they have already signalled their interest; pushing too hard when a gentler approach would do, and finally, talking **at** them instead of listening **to** them.

All of these will damage your chances of a good conclusion. However, the old-style sales cycle and its accompanying negative mental attitude can push you relentlessly in that direction. Each fail make you more dispirited and desperate; you push harder, causing even more wrong approaches, mistakes and failures.

Contrast this with the G.R.O.W.T.H.S. U.P. model, where the only approach is a natural, flowing conversation. There is no pressure to qualify, close or use a script, so the conversation proceeds naturally, as it would between two friends. There is no wrong approach, no pressure or desperation, just a N.I.C.E. C.H.A.T that leads where it leads. It's an elegantly aligned, mutually respectful dance as opposed to a solo rap.

- Another bad habit the old-style sales approach can cause is: speaking to the wrong people.

Conditioned by your targets and sales performance, and in a desperate bid to boost figures, you may find yourself cold calling and contacting anyone and everyone in a desperate attempt to set up a meeting and close a sale. This approach lacks focus, and the worse your performance gets the less focused your attempts become.

If you have a product or service aimed at a particular market, then trying to contact people too far outside of it is wasted effort and bound to fail. Knowing you are talking to the wrong people in your attempt to keep your sales figures up will affect your mental state and impact on your revenue performance and on the rest of the business, thus reducing creativity and productivity.

Contrast this to the G.R.O.W.T.H.S. U.P. model. As your only target is to have a natural conversation, a N.I.C.E. C.H.A.T., you can contact people in any way you choose. You can be more flexible in your approach, allowing focus on a target market but also the ability to try new areas without the pressure of not meeting your targets. Your only goal is the conversation; the outcome will go where it goes. So you can contact who you like, specific to your area or not, and feel free to experiment. This will lead to a greater understanding of your customer base, a wider pool and keep you positive and motivated at the same time. How refreshing.

- One of the worst bad habits to get sucked into is: the script is everything.

Though scripts have their place in old-style sales processes, they can become an inappropriate, inflexible and manipulative tool, removing the possibility of positive creativity and robbing you of the ability to really listen to your customer. They can become a crutch, which is your comfort zone. However much you dislike them, however bad you feel and however much you fail, you can get trapped into a mindset, which forces you to stick to a script and removes your personality and motivation.

In the G.R.O.W.T.H.S. U.P. model there is no script; just a series of tools, as we will show, to help you have no more and no less than a natural conversation, a N.I.C.E. C.H.A.T., which will flow in a relaxed, natural way, as in a conversation between friends.

This conversation, because you and your customer are relaxed and not combative, because there is no aggression or manipulation, becomes a normal, natural dialogue. This will lead to a mutually beneficial exchange or an understanding of each other, even if no exchange takes place. Both parties, whatever the outcome, will finish smiling and feel relaxed. You will feel motivated and positive; and because you have been in the moment and congruent, you will feel at peace with yourself, with plenty of energy to carry on the other parts of your business. Now doesn't that seem a better way?

Old thoughts and old-style thinking.

Having looked at bad habits, let us now turn to old thoughts or old-style limiting thinking, which can and does hold you back from transitioning from an old-style sales approach to the G.R.O.W.T.H.S. U.P. model.

- The first old thinking process is about having: an incorrect attitude.

We will tackle how to acquire and maintain a PMA (Positive Mental Attitude) in the next chapter. Here I want to deal with what kind of attitude the old-style sales process engenders and how important it is to understand that the G.R.O.W.T.H.S. U.P. model creates a totally different mindset. It is vitally important to embrace that new mindset and ditch the old attitude to benefit the most from the new G.R.O.W.T.H.S. U.P. model.

The incorrect attitude to ditch is the combative, aggressive, nervous one that running the old sales cycle engenders. When you go into work or get up in the morning, if you are using this process, you are already worrying about your targets, closes, objections, etc. You are in a heightened state of negative awareness expecting the worst and ready to "do battle". This mindset will affect everything you do that day and negatively affect the main area of your work, reduce creativity and impact badly on how you treat your team and fellow employees.

Contrast this with the G.R.O.W.T.H.S. U.P. model. Here, as your target is just to have a N.I.C.E. C.H.A.T. – a natural conversation – you can get up in the morning feeling relaxed and positive without the undue pressure of having to perform to unreasonable and incongruent targets.

Consequently, you feel fresher, have more energy, and because you are focused and congruent in your day, your main job will flow better. You will be more productive and you will be more relaxed with your colleagues.

All of this means that when you do implement the G.R.O.W.T.H.S. U.P. model you will be energised, relaxed and flowing, focused and in control and congruent in how you act. That will lead to natural conversations, a N.I.C.E. C.H.AT., which can lead you to mutually beneficial exchanges and revenue-enhancing conclusions.

Attitude is the basis for all. G.R.O.W.T.H.S. U.P. frees you, allowing you to have a great attitude that will positively impact you, your business and your social life.

- The next old thinking to ditch is the stressful limiting one of self-image: I am what I sell.

In the old-style sales process, the attitude it creates often means that you are forced to identify with what you sell. Failure to sell means you feel it as personal failure, seriously damaging your self-image and confidence. Over identification with a process about which you have no control of the outcome can set you up for failure; leading to loss of motivation, energy and self-esteem.

This mental attitude links to other old thoughts: fear of failure; I have to close the sale – if I don't I am a failure.

Let's tackle these together as they are inextricably linked and have the same outcome: anxiety, depression, stress, fear, failure, reduction in motivation, energy, loss of focus, productivity and connection.

When, in the old-style sales process, targets are linked to closing and volume then, because you have no control over the end result, the mental state this engenders is one of fear, stress and lowered self-image.

Even the most successful professional salespeople (which you are obviously not, otherwise you would not be reading this book) go through slumps. So it is inevitable that you, in striving to meet targets that are often out of your control and incongruent with your main focus, will be forced into over identification with the sale, the product or service. This over identification is a compensation mechanism for not being congruent and at one with the sales environment and not feeling at ease with the process. This will lead to a feeling of personal failure and anxiety when that sale does not go as expected.

The result of this failure or inability to meet your targets is a mind-set that reduces your self-image to one of victim suffering from demotivation and lethargy. Enough setbacks in an area where you are not focused and congruent will lead to you feeling as if you were "walking through glue". Your energy will vanish, your ability diminish, and productivity both in sales and in the main part of your business will be heavily reduced.

You can become trapped in a downward spiral of defeat.

The opposite occurs in the G.R.O.W.T.H.S. U.P. model.

- Your self-image is not dependent on the model. Rather, the reverse is true; the model will help boost your self-image. How? By helping you feel energised, focused, congruent and in control. This will help you stay motivated, be productive and feel great. The secret of the G.R.O.W.T.H.S. U.P. model; there is no need for the old fears. Because you are only focused on having a natural conversation – a N.I.C.E. C.H.A.T that will lead where it does, then there can be no possibility of fear of failure or worry that you have to "close" anything.

  You don't have to worry about closing as there is no close; just a natural conversation and possible exchange, if that is the natural outcome. You will not suffer a fear of failure because there is nothing to fail! Wherever the conversation goes is a success. As we will see in later chapters, if your outcome is an exchange leading to a revenue-enhancing transaction, you have won. If the conversation leads to a dialogue and the building of a relationship with no final outcome at that time, then that is also a Win-Win. The customer leaves feeling relaxed and so do you.

That will set up a positive situation for a conclusion next time; either from that customer or from someone they spoke to. As you have not been aggressive or tense, and only had a natural conversation where you have not tried to sell anything, the customer will be so surprised and relaxed at such a positive outcome they are bound to tell others. By the law of averages, one of them will want your product or service. You are building a positive reputation and potential customers will seek you out. This will lead to a revenue-enhancing transaction.

And all this in a relaxed, no-pressure positive environment. Now isn't that a better way? This is what the G.R.O.W.T.H.S. U.P. model provides. We will explore how in more detail in forthcoming chapters.

Let's now look at a few more old thoughts and old-style thinking we need to banish.

To succeed, my targets must be aggressive and push me to the limit.

This is a classic old-style sales process mind game. The old thinking is that as salespeople are inherently lazy, they will not achieve their revenue targets if they are not pushed hard. While this may or may not be true of professional salespeople, it is totally irrelevant for someone like you who has another role and has to gain new customers and revenue as well as operate in your main function as manager, entrepreneur or small business owner.

For you, who is not solely focused on sales and is definitely not lazy, forcing you to have aggressive, stressful targets will make you feel incongruent and therefore stressed and fearful. Your reduction in motivation, caused by this lack of understanding as to what drives you, will lead not to greater revenue but failure, fear and reduced productivity and output.

The best way to look at targets for you is exactly what the G.R.O.W.T.H.S. U.P. model advocates. This model has, as your targets, just having a N.I.C.E. C.H.A.T, a natural, relaxed conversation. There is no target on outcome because that will naturally flow from the dialogue. Either you will end up with an exchange and transaction where your revenue is enhanced, or a relaxed conversation that has your customer leaving happy and positive even though they have not concluded a transaction with you at this time.

The success here is that you have had the conversation, which is your target; enhanced your reputation and the customer left happy and is likely either to return and/or tell others of the positive experience. This can lead easily to more customers and greater revenue.

The model, rather than stressing you out with tough unreasonable targets which affect your productivity, motivation and self-worth, instead offers you targets that naturally fit in with your main job. Just having a N.I.C.E. C.H.A.T. is not threatening or difficult because the outcome is irrelevant. The conversation is the focus.

So for you, a hard-working manager or entrepreneur, it is easy to meet that target, succeed, stay focused, feel congruent and in control. This will lead you to be happy and to have more and more such conversations, which by the law of averages will lead to more exchanges and revenue-enhancing transactions. You will feel good, your self-worth enhanced, and the rest of your business successful because of your energised positive approach.

<u>A classic old-style thinking process taught by the classic sales process with its combative, aggressive, confrontational approach is summed up in the phrase: buyers are liars.</u>

The phrase itself sets up an assumption of confrontation and deceit. The logic goes: as buyers are liars, they will never tell you the truth about what they really want or are willing to pay. The mind-set created is that as they are lying to you, there is no reason you should not lie to them and use any trick necessary to complete the sale.

For someone who is honest and straight-forward and is not a salesperson, this approach is totally incongruent and therefore sets up mental blocks. These blocks cause fear and anger as well as resentment and drain away motivation and energy. You cannot focus, as you are not congruent while the control is, if anything, superficial. Even if you obtain the sale, you will feel drained and de-motivated by the approach you had to use and the mind-set that went against the real you.

Alternatively, the G.R.O.W.T.H.S. U.P. model provides a much more positive, relaxed and congruent approach. As the only target is having that N.I.C.E. C.HAT. and as it doesn't matter where the conversation goes, there is no reason to be anything but positive and see the exchange in a good light.

Your customers will tell you what they want, in a natural non-aggressive, non-confrontational way, so there will be no reason to lie or to expect that they would. This ensures your state is positive and open and relaxed, which in turn reflects on your customer. The conversation stays focused, you stay congruent and in control and whatever the exchange or transaction, the encounter ends with both sides, relaxed, happy and energised and in a Win-Win situation. You are ready and happy to do it all over again; the customer will return and tell their friends.

> <u>There are two final sets of old thinking I want to address.</u>
> The first combination is the attitude that: because short-term gain is what's important, let's not worry about exploiting customers. There are plenty more and even better tourists because they were set-up to be ripped off.

Professional salespeople, especially at the lower or middle end of the spectrum, have drilled into them that what counts is the deal in front of them, the objection to be qualified, the close – the deal to be had then and there. This, over time, leads to a mental attitude of short-term satisfaction over long-term gain. The mind-set is of impatience: I must have it now; there is no deferred satisfaction here. The focus is on me and my needs and my wants now, not what might happen later.

This inevitably leads to seeing the customer as sheep, to be exploited and shorn by you the wolf. The attitude is contemptuous, aggressive and dominant. The exact opposite of how most of you, non-sales people think about your customers. This attitude of seizing the reward now, never mind about the future and using any manipulative technique to do so because there will be no come back, you mistakenly assume, is magnified when dealing with tourists. The assumption in this old-style sales exploitation, is that tourists are only here for a short time, won't notice being ripped off and probably won't make a fuss, so hiking the price, or providing less for more is possible without comeback.

This thinking, though it might yield a few short-term gains, is a recipe for disaster.

The G.R.O.W.T.H.S. U.P. model is the opposite of this. Customers, all customers, are equal, respected and seen as potential long-term clients. The whole approach is based on Win-Win, building long-term relationships and reputation that will eventually and naturally yield strong, sustainable, revenue streams and customer numbers. Whoever the customer might be you are aiming for repeat business either from them, or someone they recommend is assured.

Before I leave this subject, I would like to share with you a true story to further illustrate the perils of old-style thinking. There is an early morning radio show in London on LBC that has been on the air for many years. Its

DJ, Steve Allen, often has the highest audience figures for that time slot, so we are talking numbers in seven figures at least. That's a lot of people who follow his show and listen to what he says.

Some years ago he related the story of how he had been shopping in a large electronics store, part of a well-known brand and chain. He told his listeners how he had been looking for a particular item and how badly he was treated, especially at the checkout, great radio, bad for the company.

The point is that this company's reputation was damaged so much they had to go on air with a comment – and all because the salesperson in the store had treated this customer badly. They did not know or care who he was. You never know who your customer is, so treat each one as if they have an audience of millions. That way you ensure customer service is high and your reputation remains intact. Never assume anything about your customer from their dress or purchase; you may be surprised.

The final combination of old-style thinking I wish to address is the one that states: morality is for the weak; my money is in their pocket, being nice doesn't pay bills.

This fear-based thinking engenders an aggressive, possessive attitude that reflects negative emotion on to any encounter. If you go into the sales process believing that the customer has your money and it is your right to get it whatever the cost, then the exchange will be framed as a win-lose situation. I, the salesperson, need to take the money from you the customer as its mine. And if I don't I will fail and be poor and not succeed. So, as I am under threat, any method is justified to reach my goal.

This attitude and approach will affect your voice, tone, speech patterns and body language and will, without your knowledge, transmit and be picked up by your customer. Such an approach can intimidate, unsettle, bully and therefore often fail. Even if it succeeds, the customer will feel so unsettled and negative they are unlikely to return. Indeed, they will probably complain to their friends who definitely won't come in or use your service. Finally, this attitude will leave you feeling drained, unsettled and de-motivated and will not inspire you to repeat the encounter.

The G.R.O.W.T.H.S. U.P. model, with its emphasis on a positive, stress-free, relaxed conversation, sets you up in exactly the opposite way. Rather than being scared, aggressive and possessive, you approach the customer and the conversation in an energised, relaxed, stress-free mood.

This positive framework, which allows you to be focused, congruent and in control, will also be reflected in your voice, tone and body language. As such the customer will feel unthreatened, relaxed and is much more likely to open up, stay longer, and be happy for an exchange and a revenue enhanced transaction. Even without that conclusion, they will feel they had a great conversation, a N.I.C.E. C.H.A.T., and will no doubt let their friends know what a nice experience they had. These people, in contrast to the previous approach, are more likely to seek you out and use your service or buy your product.

So in this chapter we have identified, looked at and hopefully cast aside some bad habits and old-style thinking. As we said at the beginning: in NLP there is a saying. 'If you always do what you have always done then you always get what you always got'. After reading this chapter, and having been made aware of and consequently rejecting the old, you are ready to embrace the new: specifically, new attitudes, new skills and new approaches. All of these are encapsulated in the G.R.O.W.T.H.S. U.P. model and the techniques and skills we will explore in the subsequent chapters.

To inspire you to adopt G.R.O.W.T.H.S. U.P. and embrace the new, I end this chapter with a quote used by American president, Barack Obama:

'Change will not come if we wait for some other person or some other time. We are the ones we've been waiting for. We are the change that we seek.'

Section 2 Creating the model

5 PMA – GETTING IN THE MOOD

To maximise the use of the G.R.O.W.T.H.S. U.P. model, it is best if you are in a positive frame of mind so that you are energised, relaxed, focused, congruent and in control. This is the mind state that G.R.O.W.T.H.S. U.P. encourages, supports and succeeds best in. Therefore, putting yourself into the right frame is essential before you begin to use the model. This chapter looks at one concept and several methods to get you into that state.

As we have abandoned bad habits and old-style thinking, now it is time to enter that positive state from which the model, your energy, congruence and focus will flow uninterrupted and strong.

Positive mental attitude (PMA) is the vehicle to help you achieve a positive, relaxed and congruent state and utilise the G.R.O.W.T.H.S. U.P. model to its maximum.

PMA is an idea that was first developed and introduced in 1937 by Napoleon Hill in his book *Think and Grow Rich.* Though the book never uses the phrase, it does develop the importance of positive thinking as a main factor to success. He, and W. Clement Stone, then wrote *Success Through a Positive Mental Attitude.* This book defines positive mental attitude as utilising the positive characteristics illustrated by words including: faith, hope, initiative, integrity, courage, optimism, tolerance, generosity, tact, kindliness and common sense.

Positive mental attitude (PMA) is the philosophy that having an optimistic disposition in every situation in one's life attracts positive changes and increases achievement. Adherents employ a state of mind that continues to seek, find and execute ways to win, or find a desirable outcome, regardless of the circumstances. It opposes negativity, defeatism and hopelessness. Optimism and hope are vital to the development of PMA. As quoted in the book *Optimism & pessimism implications for theory, research, and practice.* (1st edition, 2001, edited by Edward C. Chang).

So we have the origin and definition of PMA. Now how and where do we apply it to maximise PMA and obtain the most out of life in general and

G.R.O.W.T.H.S. U.P. in particular? One of the reasons this is so important to you and to the model is because the attitude you unconsciously present to the world is exactly what you will attract. So project PMA; the model works at its best if you do, and, at the same time you will feel great and full of energy. Why wouldn't you? So here's how.

In applying PMA, every situation – however difficult or trying it may seem – has a positive side if you want it to. Though you often cannot alter the situation you are in you can always decide how you wish to view that situation. In NLP terms this is known as a reframe. Let me give you two examples to start and which I have personally used.

I used to hate traffic jams. Travelling around the country, as I do and enjoying the delights, in the UK, of roads such as the M25, M6, M2 and M20 to name but a few, traffic jams are inevitable. I am sure there are motorways and roads like this where you live.

So, I used to get uptight when slowing down and stopping and seeing the car queue snaking for miles. Often it was returning from an appointment, so I was tired and just wanted to get home. After burning useless energy in frustration, anger and stress for many years, I realised how pointless this was. I could not alter the traffic jam, but I could control how I viewed it.

So I put language CDs in my car and decided that when travelling I would use the time constructively and learn a language. So when I was stuck in a jam I would listen to the CD, and instead of being frustrated at not moving, would be happy I had more time to listen and learn my lesson. The other upside is that learning a language seems to use a different part of the brain to the usual driving one so it's relaxing and takes you into another, calmer place.

I am not saying you need to learn a language; you could listen to music or an audio book, for instance. The point is, you cannot affect the traffic jam but you can affect how you feel. Stay relaxed and you will be less tired, burn less energy, reduce your stress level and get home calmer and more in control. PMA.

My other example is that I dislike shopping and used to get uptight in supermarket checkout queues. I always seemed to be behind someone who had coupons that were out of date or couldn't find their money or insisted on chatting endlessly with the person at the checkout. Again, I was getting stressed and angry at a situation I had no control over. Well, I like to observe people; I find people endlessly fascinating. So I decided that instead of getting uptight in the queue I would reframe it in my head as extra time to observe people and enjoy the experience. I turned an energy-sapping negative into a PMA.

Kipling had it right when he said: 'God give me strength to accept the things I cannot change, the courage to change the things I can, and the wisdom to know the difference.'

Let me give you some other ways to help gain and maintain your PMA.

It is said that giving is better than receiving. Well, recent research has shown that giving actually has a positive mental benefit and can have an economic one as well. Indeed, BNI, one of the world's most established business networking organisations – of which I was a member for a while – has as one of their basic quotes: 'Givers gain'. The idea being, among other things, that if you give without having any expectation of reward, and you seek success by helping others to be successful, then this will be rewarded by others giving back to you and so help you be successful.

The 2000 film *Pay it forward* had a similar theme, and is well worth watching to give you that feel good factor.

In addition, a book recently was published, which I urge you to read on this subject. *Give and Take* by Adam Grant, shows with evidence, how giving, if done correctly, can be personally enriching and financially rewarding.

So what else can help you gain and maintain PMA? Well, what about the concepts of:

Don't take things personally. This comes from the book *The Four Agreements* by Don Miguel Ruiz. As he says in his book: 'nothing other people do is because of you.' People's opinions are based on their own prejudices, beliefs and world views – not yours; so don't take it personally. This means, instead of reacting and being trapped by their negativity, you can stay positive in your own mind, free of their rubbish. Remember, AS Ruiz says: 'Your point of view is something personal to you. It's no one's truth but yours.' If you don't fear criticism because you won't take it personally then you can live your life free, positive and create and maintain your PMA. Think of yourself as having a mirror in front of you that faces outwards. Any criticism just reflects back at the person giving the criticism as it is there world view, not yours, and so cannot affect you. The mirror is your shield; criticism cannot dent it or affect your PMA.

Love yourself first before you lover others. PMA works best and is easiest when you first love yourself. You are where you need to be. You have everything in your possession to be happy, loved and fulfilled if only you realise it. Celebrate yourself, your uniqueness. You are special; you have worth and value. Love yourself completely and accept everything that you are. You are beautiful. Believe it, and most importantly, remind yourself often.

Loving yourself is an essential part of growing and nurturing yourself and making sure you take care of yourself. If you lose yourself in others and fail to love yourself then you can end up stressed, burnt out, overwhelmed and suffering from chronic tiredness and irritability. You become impatient with yourself and the others around you. The joy has gone out of your life because your core is not satisfied; you are not in love with yourself. To stay focused, congruent and in control, as we will see in the chapter on FCO[2], you need to understand loving yourself is a first and essential step.

Here are some practical methods to help you focus on you and stay in love with yourself:

When you get up in the morning take the time to greet the day with a positive thought. Rain or sun, when you get up and go to the window take a deep breath and embrace the day with thanks rather than resentment or fear. Go to the mirror and smile at yourself and say out loud: 'today will be a good day and I am worth it' or words to that effect.

Make the time to go for a walk, in the fresh air. Connect with the earth, take a deep breath, feel the breeze, feel the earth between your feet.

You are what you eat, so eat healthily and you will have more energy and feel better. Loving yourself means taking care of yourself; that includes caring about what you eat, not getting into the bad habit of junk food, rushed meals and dependence on alcohol.

Take the time, however busy your day is, to spend 15 minutes in the quiet, free from others and allow yourself the luxury of dreaming and visualising what you want in life. It will refresh and re-energise you – you deserve it. Then spend another 15 minutes doing what you love whether it's exercise or a bath, reading a book or listening to music. Just 15 minutes will be the reward that you deserve.

Steps like this slowly make you realise that you are worth it, that you are appreciated. Looking after yourself first is the basis for a happy life and PMA. Put yourself first, make yourself a priority and change begins to happen. You will feel happier, have more energy and feel more positive to the benefit of you and those around you.

Apart from not taking things personally and loving yourself, there are some other practical attitudes that you can adopt to ensure you maintain your PMA. These are mainly spelt out in the chapter on FCO² and they include the concepts of Focus, Congruence and Control. In addition remember:

Stay positive by using positive language.

Never use words like 'try' or 'maybe'; they are setting you up to fail. 'But' is a negative word; avoid it as much as possible. Also avoid words like 'always' and 'never'; they are generalisations. 'Can't' and 'won't' will sap your energy; positive people can and will. 'I choose' or 'I want' offers control and choice whereas 'I need' or 'I should' traps you into obedience or victim-like feelings.

Do not harbour anger, resentment, and judgment. Forgiveness is the most positive, energizing feeling you can have.

Hanging on to negative emotions like anger or resentment will drain your energy and block you from moving forward. To let go of these emotions acknowledge the feelings associated with the initial negative experience. Accept them and then let them go, as they no longer serve you. Forgive those who caused them; this will free you from the shackles they bind you in and allow you to get rid of the negative anchor that is a weight around your soul, freeing you to move forward in a positive frame of mind.

Surround yourself with supportive, positive people and lose those who criticise you or put you down.

Surround yourself with people who are positive influences: people who speak the truth and support you. Increase your circle to include people who are further ahead in personal and professional development than you are. Disassociate yourself from negative people who impede your progress.

<u>You have control over what you think and do.</u>

Whatever the outside circumstances you have total control over how you react and deal with it. Use PMA, stay optimistic, and you will have more energy to maintain that control and exercise it in a positive way and so obtain the most out of any situation however challenging it might be.

Finally, be content with where you are today and don't make the mistake of putting off being happy because you are waiting for the right moment to shine. Sometimes it takes a conscious effort to enjoy the journey.

Not everyone woke up this morning and not everyone will go to bed tonight. Life has no guarantees. Every minute you are living is a blessing that has to be experienced in the moment. It's not always easy, but it's always an option – a choice; your choice.

Some meditation resources to help you boost your PMA

PMA Meditation on YouTube: https://youtu.be/Jus46TEE5t4

PMA Affirmations on YouTube: https://youtu.be/r1BZYyBvPN8

6 IT'S TIME TO SMILE

The first of our main acronyms to help us with the G.R.O.W.T.H.S. U.P. Model is S.M.I.L.E.

S.M.I.L.E. stands for:

- S – start with a smile
- M – make eye contact
- I – individualise
- L – look, listen, lead
- E – engage

We all know smiling relaxes others and makes you feel more positive. However, as applied to the G.R.O.W.T.H.S. U.P. project, I am going to unlock the hidden secret behind your smile to maximise your natural encounter. Intrigued? Well read on:

[S]MILE – START WITH THE SMILE

The "S" stands for "Start with a Smile". Though this may seem obvious, it is amazing how many people forget to begin their encounter and their conversation with one of these. Why is this important? Well, smiling has several positive effects on both the person smiling and the recipient of that smile. Smiles are contagious and developed through a process of evolution. Seeing someone smile at you prevents you using the muscles you need to frown. That's why smiling is so contagious. Think about how much children smile (up to 400 times a day) and how much you smile when you are with them and how good you feel. Is it the Mona Lisa's smile that makes that painting so popular? Many people think it is and they smile when they look at it.

When our brain feels good and tells us to smile, we smile and tell our brain, it feels good – and the loop continues both for ourselves and the people we are smiling at as in the diagram below.

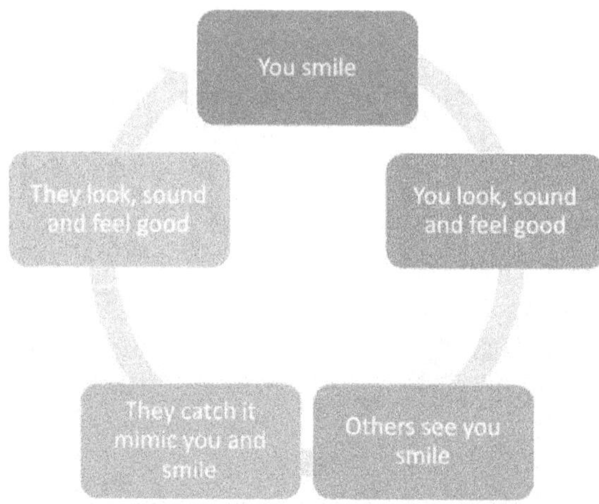

According to Ron Gutman, founder and CEO of the company Interactive Health, one smile stimulates the brain as much as 2,000 bars of chocolate. Or, that smiling can be as stimulating as receiving up to 16,000 pounds sterling in cash.

Smiling reduces stress by suppressing cortisol and adrenaline while boosting positive hormones such as endorphins. So, smiling makes you feel good, helps you be successful, reduces stress, helps you live longer and is catching. Yes, live longer.

Two well-known studies managed to equate how much someone smiled and their success in life and longevity:

- The "yearbook study" tracked the lives of women who had the best smiles in yearbook photos compared to the rest. Women who smiled the most lived happier lives, had happier marriages and fewer setbacks.

- The "baseball card study" found a clear link between how big a smile someone made on a baseball card photo and how long they would live. The people who smiled the most turned out to live seven years longer than those who didn't.

Still not convinced? Then check out this Ron Gutman video on smiling

https://youtu.be/U9cGdRNMdQQ

Smiling affects not just how you look, but also how you sound. Because of the physical movements of various muscles when you smile and the accompanying physiological and psychological changes, this has a direct effect on your voice. I am sure you have heard the old cliché, 'smile even when on the phone.' Well it works. When you smile, your vocal cords change, your voice becomes gentler and richer and your mood is affected – and in a feedback loop that affects your voice.

So as we shall see, to have that N.I.C.E. C.H.A.T. – the natural conversation that the

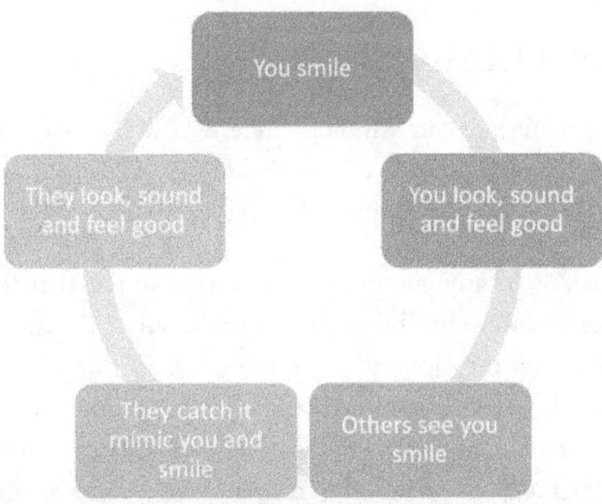

model is all about – smiling is the first step to looking, sounding and feeling good; and to transfer that feeling to your customer. It's a real Win-Win.

Also, it's important because if you have a nervous, shy or unhappy client, the act of smiling actually reduces someone's threat levels and their fear. Subconsciously, most people responding to a smile feel that someone smiling at them will not attack them. Usually this is true.

If you don't believe how powerful this is, try this experiment.

Next time you are walking down a street in town and coming toward you is an elderly or frail-looking person, or someone you think might be nervous, keep your face neutral till you are a few feet away from them. Then give them a genuine smile. Their faces will transform from uncertainty to pleasure and most times they will smile back. Smiling is so powerful.

Finally, if you struggle to smile try this exercise from researcher Andrew Newberg:

'We just asked a person, before they engage in a conversation with someone else, to visualise someone they deeply love, or recall an event that brought them deep satisfaction and joy. It's such an easy exercise, and we train people to do it in our workshops.'

Then when you do have your natural conversation you will find it easier to smile, and because it's catching, your customer will relax and smile back.

S[M]ILE – MAKE EYE CONTACT

So, having established our winning smile, we now move on to the second part of the formula, the "M" for making eye contact, which is not as straightforward as you might imagine.

It is essential, as in any genuinely natural encounter, that to pay attention, establish trust – and to be able to get the most out of the meeting – you must make good strong but not excessive eye contact. Too much eye contact is instinctively felt to be hostile, rude, and condescending. Do this in a business environment and it may also be seen as a deliberate intent to dominate, intimidate, belittle, or make the recipient of the eye contact feel at a disadvantage. Think of how, in many armies, the drill sergeant stares into somebody's face while instructing them, and how uncomfortable this feels just to watch, let alone experience.

In contrast, if there is not enough eye contact then the person can come over as insincere unprepared or dodgy. The correct amount of eye contact produces a feeling of mutual interaction and congruence as it engenders feelings of like and trust. This will vary with gender, personality, situations, and cultural differences, as we shall see later.

Where gender is concerned, it is known that women look more at those they are talking to than do men. If you watch the two genders in conversation you will often notice that women prefer face-to-face conversations, while men are often happy to talk standing side-by-side.

In the West, as an average, direct eye contact ranging from 30% to 60% of the conversation should produce the correct environment for a conversation as eye contact produces a powerful, subconscious sense of connection. Obviously, more eye contact is necessary when you are listening and less when you are speaking.

It is worth noting that we limit eye contact when we talk about something we feel guilty about or is embarrassing to us. When we are upset, stressed or depressed, and when we are internalising, we reduce our eye contact as well.

In contrast, when dealing with powerful people or people we like or look up to, we increase our eye contact. It is clear that in emotionally intense, intimate, conversations we look at each another more frequently and maintain the gaze for longer periods of time. Think of two lovers talking and how frequent and long their eye contact is. The rule we work by subconsciously is the greater the eye contact, the closer the relationship.

Though the bubble of personal safety and special happiness varies by culture, with it being further apart in the West and smaller in the East as a general rule, it is still true that to protect that personal space we will avoid eye contact in crowded trains, lifts or buses. We either keep staring at the door, as in a lift, or avert our gaze and look above people in a train or bus. Or we use a distraction mechanism like reading a paper or looking at our tablet or smart phone – anything to avoid eye contact. Studies show that in crowded cities people avoid eye contact more than in rural environments as their personal space comes under greater attack.

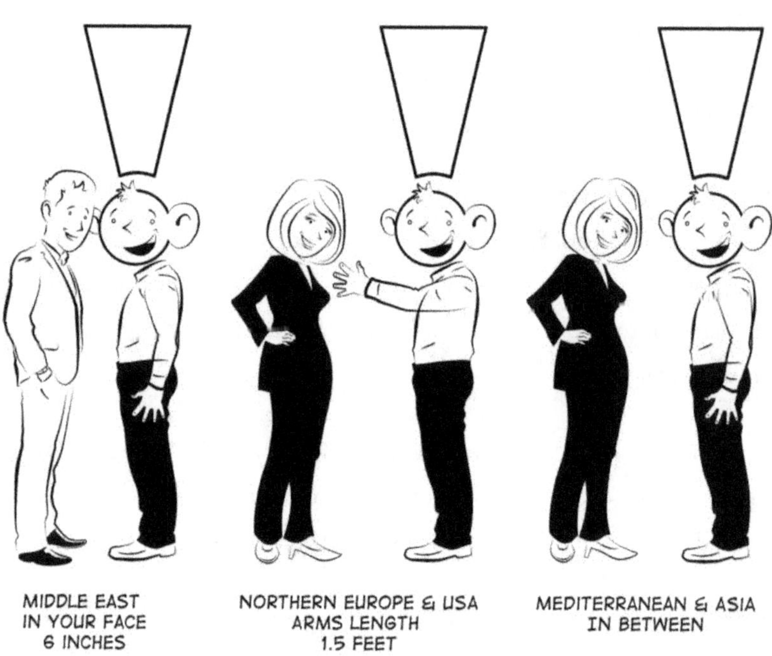

Staff often lower their eyes when their superior asks a tricky question or addresses them, though this is culturally biased as we shall see. How frustrating it is when waiters avoid eye contact, sending us the signal that they are too busy to attend to us now.

If a presenter or speaker at a networking event, business conference or in a group situation actively seeks out eye contact when talking, they are assessed to be more believable, confident and competent.

The need for eye contact originates from almost the moment we are born; babies soon seek eye contact with their mothers, for example. This link and how it develops means that in our minds we associate strong eye contact with innocence and trust. So, failure to generate such eye contact can lead to assumptions of guilt, or of having something to hide, even though that might not be the case. Auditory-biased individuals, for instance, make less eye contact than visually-biased ones. Autistic children and adults often struggle to make eye contact.

However, there is something else to consider. Eye contact is also culturally dependent.

For example, Western cultures such as Europe including the UK, the USA and Australia are all fairly similar in respect to when and where eye contact is appropriate. Eye contact is expected in Western culture; it is a basic essential to a social interaction, which shows a person's interest and engagement with your conversation. In Western cultures eyes are considered to show the central point of a person's focus. So if somebody doesn't give any eye contact during a conversation, it may be considered insulting. Many people would take this to mean that they weren't interested, and take their wandering eyes as a sign of distraction. In other, more formal, circumstances in Western cultures a lack of eye contact can be seen in another way. For example, in an interview situation, strong eye contact by the interviewee is seen as a sign of self-belief, whereas a lack of eye contact is seen as a lack of confidence.

In Middle Eastern cultures however, eye contact is less common, and considered less appropriate than in Western cultures. There are strict gender rules whereby women should not make too much eye contact with men as it could be misconstrued as a romantic interest and vice versa. Muslims often lower their gaze and try not to focus on the opposite sex's features except for the hands and face. Lustful glances to those of the opposite sex, young or adult, are also prohibited.

In Asian cultures they place great importance on respect. Hierarchies are much more visible in their society than in Western cultures, and their social behaviours mirror this. In countries such as China and Japan, eye contact is not considered an essential to social interaction and instead is often considered inappropriate. In such an authoritarian culture it is believed that subordinates shouldn't make steady eye contact with their superiors. As adults, the Japanese lower their eyes when speaking to a superior as a gesture of respect. For example, students are discouraged from making eye contact with their professors as it can be interpreted as a sign of disrespect. Similarly a daughter will point her eyes downwards when her father is speaking to her as a sign of politeness and respect.

In African and Latin American cultures, on the other hand, they remain hierarchical. In many circumstances intense eye contact is seen as aggressive, confrontational and extremely disrespectful.

So as we can see, making eye contact is vital when you have your natural conversation. Get it right, and with the rest of your S.M.I.L.E., the N.I.C.E. C.HA.T. and staying on right PA.T.H. while breaking through the N.O.I.S.E. and utilising FCO², you will find the model allows you that relaxed, natural and successful customer-increasing, revenue-generating experience you so want.

SM[I]LE – INDIVIDUALISE

Let us continue with our S.M.I.L.E. formula and now look at the "I" that stands for **individualising** the experience. Unlike in old-style sales processes and formulas where you almost feel you have to adapt the customer to the script or process, in the G.R.O.W.T.H.S. U.P. model, because we are concentrating on just having a natural conversation, as you would with a friend, there is no script or rule.

We offer a series of tools that give you the flexible skill to maximise each encounter as an individual exchange. The person in front of you is someone you want to chat to and help, not a mark, a pigeon, sheep to be sheared or a dummy to be taken advantage of.

As that is your mindset – as you see the person in front of you, or in communication with you as an individual – you relate to them as a person not an object. You empathise with them as an equal, happy to help and guide, not control or fear. This positive, relaxed mindset, which the model engenders, means you will have a joyously successful encounter whatever the outcome. The encounter is the goal, not the outcome, which will happen naturally and positively.

Focus on the person and the moment. By having your focus on the customer and having that individual conversation with someone you want to understand and help, you can avoid the distraction of outside pressures or rigid frameworks or scripts. Go with the flow and let your natural energy and conversation embrace both of you in a generous, giving and positive atmosphere. This is the environment most likely to create a new customer and a revenue-enhancing conclusion and transaction.

SMI[L]E – LOOK, LISTEN, LEAD

Let us now turn to the "L" in S.M.I.L.E., which actually stands for three things: Look closely, Listen intently and Lead gently.

First, "Look closely". This is to remind you that your focus, as we have said, is solely on the person you are engaging with at that moment, in that space. You should place all your energy on looking at them, engaging with them and – free from distractions – build a natural conversation in an atmosphere that is friendly, relaxed and positive.

Now "Listen intently". Again, free from distraction in a stimulating and joyful atmosphere, you might consider what I call the "Active Listening Response Technique" or being ALERT. There is a great difference between hearing and listening. I want to introduce you to "Lert" who is going to remind you how to apply this technique.

This is Lert. To be A-LERT you have to apply

Active **L**ist**e**ning **R**esponse **T**echnique. It will change you from passive to pro-active. It will focus your attention inward, remove distraction, enhance your power of perception, allow rapid and accurate responses and deliver assertive solutions.

All you have to do be like Lert is to: close your eyes [if on the phone], slow your breathing so it is deeper, physically listen [it's an act of will], concentrate all your mind on listening and ignore outside stimuli. Be like a sniper and focus only on the person you are in front of or talking to.

On the telephone this means it allows you to filter outside distraction while receiving a more complete mental picture. You will be able to feel the emotional state of the person on the phone by more easily assessing the background and context they are talking in. This will allow you to answer more quickly and more accurately and help you resolve problems more effectively.

In face-to-face encounters it helps you by making you concentrate on the other person. Physically listening prevents unnecessary chatter allowing a focus on their needs, not your want. By being A- LERT You will be able to ask relevant meaningful questions and reply to the responses precisely and powerfully.

So being A-LERT and applying the **A**ctive **L**ist**e**ning **R**esponse **T**echnique will allow you to listen intently, have a natural, powerful and meaningful conversation and help you S.M.I.L.E. even more effectively.

Finally in this section, the last "L" stands for "Lead gently".

This is to remind you that unlike the aggressive, dominating sales culture where you are there to win a war, qualify objections and force a close (all aggressive leading techniques), in the G.R.O.W.T.H.S. U.P. model we are there solely to have a genuine, relaxed conversation in which we listen to our customer and help them solve their problems. This will lead to a mutually beneficial conclusion and transaction, if that is the natural outcome. If not, then you will have had a relaxed exchange, which can be built upon for the future.

That is done not by short-term aggressive and manipulative Win-Lose behaviour, but by engaging in a gentle, leading process that will end up as a Win-Win for both of you. Not just now, but in the future too. The atmosphere you should create, I would suggest, is summed up perfectly in the quote below.

So, don't glance or hear without understanding or lead aggressively; that's for old-style sales not our natural approach. G.R.O.W.T.H.S. U.P. takes you down the path of gentle, moral, congruent and joyful success. Embrace it and feel your energy flow.

**Don't walk in front of me ; I may not follow.
Don't walk behind me;
I may not lead.
Just Walk beside me
and be my friend
-Albert Camus**

SMIL[E] – ENGAGE

The final letter in this formula is "E" for engage. This is the letter that brings it all together and summarises how powerful your S.M.I.L.E. really is.

Now you have smiled, made eye contact, individualised your focus while looking, listening and leading the customer gently to what they need.

Now you can totally engage with them in a natural, flowing conversation, grounded in the moment, without distraction, fear or resistance. This relaxed dialogue will keep you and them focused, positive, relaxed and engaged and inevitably lead to a hassle-free exchange or revenue-enhancing transaction.

Remember to smile. It really works, and the hidden formula makes it even more powerful to use and to benefit from.

7 NOW JUST BE N.I.C.E.

The second of our main acronyms to help us with the G.R.O.W.T.H.S. U.P. model is N.I.C.E.

N.I.C.E. stands for:

- N – natural
- I – individual
- C – clarify alignment
- E – exchange

In our use of this model, as we have mentioned, we are creating the environment conducive to a relaxed, natural conversation where the target is the conversation, not the end result or the need to close or secure a deal. As part of this process, once you have learnt to S.M.I.L.E., you need to add to that having a N.I.C.E. C.H.A.T.

The first element to this is just being N.I.C.E.

In this formula, to further help you develop your G.R.O.W.T.H.S. U.P. model, we look at the elements that help that natural conversation develop and flow in a relaxed and positive environment.

The "N" in N.I.C.E. stands for: being Natural and involves the following elements:

- trust
- enthusiasm (genuine)
- alignment
- being relaxed
- genuine
- curiousity
- openness
- PMA

All of these are naturally present in a normal conversation you would have with a friend or colleague. Indeed, their absence indicates you are probably slipping back into the old-style formulae and sales scripts or processes and abandoning the natural conversation that the G.R.O.W.T.H.S. U.P. model advocates.

Being natural requires an element of trust between both parties in the conversation. If you are having that chat in a mutually relaxed, non-aggressive environment then it is easy to build and maintain trust, as there is no hint of manipulation, falseness or pushy sales technique. Indeed, the problem with old-style sales techniques is that to try and build that essential trust, they often need to use artificial scripts and processes, which means the trust never exists or is fragile and easily broken.

Similarly, when you are having a normal chat with a friend or acquaintance, the more you engage with them in a mutually stimulating, engaging and interesting discussion, the more your genuine energy and enthusiasm grows and radiates. It becomes infectious and mutually supportive so that both of you are having an enthusiastic, energised and positive dialogue. This genuine enthusiasm is only there in a natural conversation. In a scripted or manipulative sales pitch, the enthusiasm is forced and is often seen through. The atmosphere has an edge to it and flows differently. This is often picked up by the customer, which leads to distrust with the result that the discussion goes nowhere and both parties leave feeling unhappy.

As a natural extension of enthusiasm, you will find that alignment between you and your customer happens naturally when you're having that nice chat, that natural conversation. Alignment is in body language, voice tone and the words used.

You will know when you are aligned because the conversation will flow smoothly and the atmosphere will stay positive and relaxed. This is the reverse of a scripted or manipulative conversation that you would have if you were using the old-style sales process.

Being relaxed is another feature of the natural environment that you will be working in. You are having a natural conversation and not using a sales script that you are trying to remember or manipulative techniques that you are trying to utilise. So you can stay relaxed and the whole focus of your attention and conversation is on your customer. As you don't have to worry about targets, closes or objections and can just have a nice chat, your natural conversation flows smoothly.

Whatever the outcome, both you and the customer will remain relaxed and positive ensuring the possibility of another exchange either with them or with somebody they recommend. It's the ultimate Win-Win situation: no pressure, just a positive, relaxed, natural conversation, exchange and possible transaction.

It is extremely hard for salespeople, either on the phone or face-to-face, to sound genuine, as they often have to resort to scripts or processes designed to manipulate their customers. This lack of being genuine, however hard they try to fake it, is usually picked up by the customer and immediately causes resistance to – and suspicion of – the person talking to them.

In contrast, being natural as part of the G.R.O.W.T.H.S. U.P. model allows you to be completely genuine. You are there to have a nice chat, no more. As there is no need for manipulative technique or script you can relax and be completely genuine with your customer. This will put them at ease and they will respond naturally and openly to you, making the exchange more pleasant and the transaction more likely

Being genuine, enthusiastic, aligned and relaxed allows you to stay natural by also encouraging openness and curiosity. Just as in a conversation with a friend or stranger, having an attitude of friendly openness and curiosity will engage your customer in a conversation that is interesting, revealing and relaxed. By asking questions and being genuine, open and curious, you will find out about your customer's needs and wants in a positive, calm way. This will allow you, without manipulation or objection handling, to understand exactly what they need and how they feel, and help you serve them with the right product or service in a congruent, focused, accurate and professional manner.

The final element of being natural – PMA – we dealt with in chapter five. A

Positive Mental Attitude will always be beneficial when dealing with others.

So remember this is a natural conversation similar to that you would have with a friend or acquaintance. These elements should be naturally present and will help you relax into a naturally flowing conversation, a positive exchange and revenue-enhancing transaction.

The second element of just being N.I.C.E. is the "I" which stands for the individual. In this case you are an individual and your customer is also an individual and not just another face or target; a human being to be nurtured not a mark to be conned.

This letter in N.I.C.E. is to remind you that you are you not some false high-pressure salesperson or manipulator. Using the talents and skills you have and have learnt in this book, you can be genuine and congruent; an individual not a parrot or copy of some other person or technique.

This also allows you, the individual, to relate to your customer as an individual. A mistake made by high-pressure salespeople is that they look at each customer as just one more battle; and are affected badly if they feel they have lost the previous ones by not closing or reaching their targets. As such they approach each new encounter by looking back on the failure of the past and see not an individual in front of them but a faceless battle they have to win.

You on the other hand, using your nice, natural, approach, respond to them as an individual. Each encounter is fresh and new. All you are doing is having a nice chat, a natural conversation, and so you feel fresh and positive and look forward to each customer. That means you actually look at them as a unique person, one to nurture and serve rather than someone you need to battle. You are energised and relaxed as opposed to drained and stressed. This guarantees a better conversation and a positive exchange – just by being individual.

The individual part of N.I.C.E. is about avoiding formulas and standard responses or thought processes and instead going with the flow of the conversation. The G.R.O.W.T.H.S. U.P. model teaches you these natural techniques and skills to help you avoid formulaic responses and instead respond as an individual who has internalised the natural skills we offer as human beings.

Finally, as an individual, let me highlight the NLP saying and concept that 'the map is not the territory'. This is to remind you that people are individuals and as such are far more than any labels or tags that may be stuck to them. People are not generalisations; they are unique and individual as you are.

The next letter in N.I.C.E. is the "C", which signifies the need to clarify. Clarity will ensure that your nice chat stays on the right lines and achieves the objectives both you and the customer desire: clarity in alignment of discussion, reflecting your customer's language, posture, voice tone and clarity of your customer's needs. This is about making sure that you align your discussion to focus clearly on the customer thus avoiding tension or misunderstanding.

This clarity ensures a natural stress-free conversation as you are focusing on what the customer wants, not what you want to push or provide (unlike normal sales techniques and scripts).

There is an NLP saying. 'Energy flows where attention goes.' So clarity, because of your attention, will also ensure an energised, stress-free and clear conversation.

The clarity is about reflecting back the customer's language and needs so they feel at ease. ***This is reviewed in detail in the chapter on "Being on the right PA.T.H." and the subject of body language is considered in more detail in the chapter "Applying G.R.O.W.T.H.S. U.P.".***

In summary, then, clarity of language ensures a tension-free chat while clarity of body posture ensures a stress-free, sympathetic environment. Clarity of tone, and of voice, ensures the conversation is clear, unambiguous and stays on the right path for both the customer and yourself.

The final letter in N.I.C.E. is the "E" for exchange, and this letter highlights the fact that the natural conversation, the nice chat, is all about an exchange of some sort. No exchange will lead both the customer and you to feel incomplete and uncomfortable.

The exchange does not have to be monetary though it can and often will lead to a revenue-enhancing transaction as a completion of the exchange. That, however, is not your focus; your goal is a positive exchange that builds for the future and leaves both you and the client feeling positive relaxed and happy.

The "E" is to remind you that a **nice** conversation must end with some form of mutually beneficial exchange. Both of you want and are looking for a conclusion; with it you both feel relaxed and satisfied. Without it there is tension as both sides feel there is something missing.

The exchange does not have to be money paid for a service or product; that is just one ending, a financial transaction between the customer and yourself. The exchange may be no more than a natural conversation where there is an exchange of views. Perhaps you understand the customer's needs clearly but are unable to fulfil those needs. In this case the exchange is the information and that the customer understands the service or product you provide. As you are not pushing for a close, the exchange of ideas and information is sufficient. The customer will feel relaxed and even though they have not bought your product or service, will go away knowing you listened, treated them as an individual, and understood their need.

You may recommend another solution to them – another company that might have the product or service they need – or just listen and acknowledge that in this case you are unable to fulfil their needs, but would be happy to do so on another occasion. The customer will be so impressed with you not pushing aggressively for a sale, as most sales people would. And even more, having treated them with decency and respect, they are bound to tell others. More than likely one of those will contact you and a transaction will then take place. You are not working just for the moment, you are always building for the future, and a natural exchange will always help you do this.

Use this approach and you customer will always be satisfied even if all you had was that nice chat – that natural conversation. The exchange will then leave them feeling you have listened and tried to help. This exchange is treating them with respect, listening and caring. They feel satisfied and positive; you feel relaxed, refreshed and energised, ready for the next individual to talk to.

So with that in mind, make the exchange Win-Win. That way both of you feel you have received value and your customer will inevitably come back again or tell others. The exchange is an **equal** exchange of value, whether financial or of ideas and understanding.

Now we know how to be N.I.C.E. and stay natural and individual while maintaining clarity and ensuring an exchange takes place; next we need to develop that concept further by linking it to our next acronym C.H.A.T. Together, as will be made clear, having a N.I.C.E. C.H.A.T. will enhance your use of the G.R.O.W.T.H.S. U.P. model and help you increase customers and revenue.

8 SO LET'S C.H.A.T.

The third of our main acronyms to help us with the G.R.O.W.T.H.S. U.P. model is C.H.A.T.

C.H.A.T. stands for:

- C – clarify your need
- H – highlight values
- A – agree exchange
- T – tie up the transaction

This acronym builds on the N.I.C.E. part of the chat we have just looked at, so that together they give you a powerful way to understand and remember the skills and approach you need to operate the G.R.O.W.T.H.S. U.P. model and have that natural conversation. With that in mind let's look at each part of the formula in more detail:

The first letter in C.H.A.T. is the "C" which stands for clarifying needs. In the N.I.C.E. formula, the "clarify" is concerned with being aligned and having clarity in the conversation. Here we consider taking that clarity further by clarifying the customer's need in a natural, relaxed way. We are looking to ascertain why the customer is here and/or why they are talking to you specifically.

How do we do this in the most natural and relaxed way? Rather than use stilted scripts or aggressive, manipulative questioning as advocated in some sales techniques, the G.R.O.W.T.H.S. U.P. model utilises the natural flow of dialogue to gain the answers to help you serve your customer best. We use open questions, which is a more relaxed way of eliciting information. These consist of the five "Ws": who, what, when, where, why, and how. I would in certain circumstances add a sixth "W" – "which".

The other gain in using this model is that it avoids the worst retail question used by so many: 'Can I help you?' This question is a closed and not open one and risks the answer 'No', which prevents any natural conversation from proceeding. Using the six "Ws" we avoid this and obtain the information we need to help the customer make the best choice.

By using this natural formula in a different order you can genuinely tap into exactly **which** item or service is of interest. Once that is understood I would ascertain **why** they are looking for this particular product or service. Once that is clear we can find out **what** it is specifically or generally that is of interest in that item or service. It is also important you understand the pressure they may be under as to **when** they need the item and **when** it needs to be delivered or provided.

Another area of need you must clarify is **who** this item or service is for. It is vital you understand this as otherwise you may be explaining the wrong feature or benefit to the customer you are dealing with. Once that is established it is useful to know, if relevant, **where** they will use the product or service. Will it be at home, or at work; locally or abroad? All of this information will affect how you serve your customer best and offer the best product or service relevant to their real need or want.

Finally in this first part of your chat, you need to confirm **how** they want to proceed. **How** do they wish to pay, if you are at that stage; **how** do they want to collect or have the goods or service delivered?

These open questions should be asked slowly and in a relaxed, interested and focused manner. You are not interrogating your customer; you are treating them with respect and interest, helping to understand their needs better so you can make sure you can serve them best.

This method, linked to the S.M.I.L.E. and N.I.C.E. has guided you naturally and in a relaxed way to clarify your customer needs, allowing you to focus clearly on that. You have avoided the use of scripts or other artificial sales gimmicks and still acquired the information you need naturally and in a positive, collaborative atmosphere.

Having clarified the need, we now need to move on to the second letter in C.H.A.T. – **the "H", which stands for highlighting value.**

Value is defined as: 'The regard that something is held to deserve; the importance, worth, or usefulness of something.'

Most commercial entities usually also offer what is known as a "Value Proposition". That is: a statement that summarises why a customer should buy a product or use a service. This statement should convince them that one particular product or service will add more value or better solve a problem than other similar ones. This statement is used to target customers who will benefit most from using that specific product or service. The ideal value proposition is concise and appeals to the customer's strongest decision-making impulses.

Remember value and a customer's decision making is subjective and is based on assumptions, desires, previous experience and perception of the product and environment. It is also to do with common rules we buy into but which really don't exist. For example, the value of money is only what we accept it to be, not its intrinsic value. In the end the value of stocks and shares is subjective. The price of a product rarely reflects the cost of production. For example, an expensive watch or bag, or luxury item, is priced because of its name or appeal, not its cost to produce. At the other end of the spectrum, a £2 shirt in a supermarket. Do we consider how it could have been made that cheaply and what manufacturing techniques might have been used to get that price?

With that in mind consider that here we are looking at ensuring your customer has a reason to purchase the product or service from you. They are looking for exactly what you would look for, which is good value. And in this section we look at how you can naturally highlight the value to them of your product or service.

So why not start with what you would want to know about the service or product, talk about that benefit and see if that resonates with your customer. If that benefit resonates with your customer then continue along this path; amplifying the detail and always asking the customer what they think so you maintain focus and focus on the relevant value to them. There is no point stressing the value of, say, a washing machine running quietly if the person actually has a priority for the size of load and that is what they consider good value.

Naturally in your relaxed chat, then follows why isit worthwhile to that person and what they will get out of it. Remember this is a N.I.C.E. C.H.A.T. with an individual and unique person who you wish to serve, respect and help. Their value is personal and so your questions and responses should not be highlighting what you wish to push but what they need for the product or service to **add value** to their life and be **of value** to purchase. Concentrate on that, gently and respectfully, and your customer will move through the exchange to a transaction that is revenue-enhancing.

The conversation should then flow naturally into whether this product or service has the features they need. Remember, you are not selling anything; you are merely finding out if this product or service suits your customer, a bit like a well-fitting glove or nice woolly sweater. If they feel good about the product or service at this stage because the fit is there, then you can easily illustrate the advantages relevant to them and the value will be clear.

However, if the product or service is not a good fit or does not suit, that is also OK because your target is the conversation not the sale. You have demonstrated value by your approach, concern and focus; your respectful treating of them as an individual. You have found that out in a relaxed way and can either offer another product or service that will fit, or more importantly, if you don't have one, don't worry.

Thank them for their time and if you can point them in the right direction, even if it's to a competitor, do so. You will lose nothing by this and the customer will remember your honesty and genuine help and will come back to you for something else. More than that, because this honesty and naturalness is so unusual they will tell their friends and colleagues. Your reputation will be enhanced and you will get more customers and exposure.

So not selling, just chatting and being honest, will reward you and you will feel good as well. You have highlighted your value and even though the product or service might not have been the right fit, your value as an honest trustworthy person has been established and you have sown a seed, which can bring immense value in the future. It is the future that is the goal; building up your reputation and brand, adding value with every N.I.C.E. C.H.A.T. whatever the outcome.

Having highlighted value, we can now move smoothly into the next letter in C.H.A.T. **The "A", which stands for "Agree an exchange".**

This is relatively simple, yet in selling people get stressed, find this hard and so avoid it. In old-style sales techniques the exchange is associated with targets, qualifying the objections, closing the deal, asking for money; a process of questions and requests even a lot of professional salespeople hate and fear. Because they fear this it often colours their whole discussion and some even forget or avoid asking for the exchange because they are so stressed out and sure they will fail. It's a mind-sapping, energy draining activity. What a waste of effort.

In contrast, the G.R.O.W.T.H.S. U.P. model is about energising and relaxing you by having a naturally flowing conversation: your N.I.C.E. C.H.A.T. Remember, you are not selling anything. Your target is your conversation, whatever the outcome, and an exchange is always possible without pressure or stress. That will make it happen. At this stage, you have clarified your customer's need and highlighted the values. Purchase or not, your customer wants to proceed with an exchange.

In fact, your customer needs it. Both sides want a conclusion. Your natural chat will ensure that conclusion is Win-Win. As it has been a natural, relaxed conversation rather than a high-pressure sales pitch, both of you are relaxed; the customer wants what you are offering and you are happy to offer it to them. This might be an actual purchase or transaction or it might be the offering of value, as discussed before, of an honest, trusted exchange that will leave them feeling positive, happy and relaxed.

That is the value you have offered, the exchange that has taken place. This means you will have a Win-Win exchange, which will set the scene for future success. The conclusion of the exchange, needed to satisfy both you and the customer, is either tying up the transaction, which we will look at next, or thanking the customer for their time. You may have offered another solution, even if it involves a competitor, or just ensured they have had enough time and space to finish chatting to you without feeling rushed or pressured into buying. You have given them all the time they need and they leave happy and satisfied because even without a purchase both sides have exchanged value, as we discovered before.

Both sides feel good, relaxed, happy and satisfied. That means both sides can smile and the relationship, built on trust and natural flow, has reached a natural conclusion. This means that both sides have built bridges for more exchanges IN the future – a Win-Win.

The last letter in C.H.A.T. flows naturally from the previous ones. We have clarified need, highlighted value and agreed an exchange. Now, where relevant, we are going to use **the "T" to Tie up the transaction**.

We have just established that by clarifying the need and highlighting the value, if this value resonates with the customer, they will want an exchange – just as you do – that involves a purchase. In this case, we now have to ensure that this exchange is brought to a natural and final conclusion by tying up the transaction. That is the exchange between two parties in business where mutual value is established and a need identified that can be satisfied by your product or service.

There are of course some basic guidelines to ensure the transaction takes place. As you have not forced the customer to this point by pressure, scripts or manipulative techniques, the customer is ready to engage in a transaction willingly and even joyfully.

'**People love to buy but hate being sold to**.' This is exactly the situation your N.I.C.E. C.H.A.T., your natural conversation, has brought them to. So instead of the classic salesperson, dreading the close because of the pressure and atmosphere they have created, you, using the G.R.O.W.T.H.S. U.P. model, can ask for the transaction because your customer willingly and happily wants to buy. Indeed they may ask for the transaction to take place before you even get to mention it, as this is the natural consequence of your N.I.C.E. C.HA.T.

Consider this. It is essential that you both gain satisfaction by a clear conclusion because both of you want no loose ends and both of you want the transaction tied up. If the clarity of the transaction is not there then the customer will leave frustrated and you will feel disappointed. Your customer wants you to conclude the transaction. So ensure that you tie up any paperwork and where relevant obtain a signature and confirm payment and commitment. Your customer needs you to do this at this stage as they have happily agreed to the transaction and feel emotionally that they need completion. This is something to celebrate, unlike in old sales techniques where asking for the money or signature is often feared or avoided.

Once this is done, as a natural conclusion to your chat, one which both of you want, then you can both feel warm and satisfied knowing your natural flow, your **N.IC.E. C.H.A.T.** has taken both of you to a great place where both of you wanted to be – feeling good, feeling the benefit.

You have a satisfied customer not just for now but also for the future and you feel satisfied relaxed and so good. So good that all you want is to do it again. What a contrast to those poor, aggressive, tired and drained salespeople.

Smiling and having a nice chat yields results, removes stress and generates revenue and customers both for now and the future. No selling, just a natural conversation where the object, the goal, is just to have a natural nice chat. If you and your customer establish the mutual value of the product or service, everything flows to a successful transaction. If not, then you have had a relaxed chat, added value, and both of you can go on your way feeling satisfied and positive, feeling good. No sales, no pressure; the goal always achieved is to just chat.

Even in this case, transactions will follow naturally when they are supposed to. And as you are under no pressure you will find results occur more rapidly and easily than you could imagine. That is how you ensure your G.R.O.W.T.H.S. U.P.

9 BREAKING THROUGH THE N.O.I.S.E.

Having looked at how to S.M.I.L.E. and have a N.I.C.E. C.H.A.T., we now need to understand about a barrier to our natural conversation; something that might prevent us from communicating effectively, positively, clearly and accurately. This is the barrier we call "Noise". It is something that distorts understanding in a conversation.

By being aware of and learning how to break through the noise, we can ensure an effective and natural conversation where both parties understand exactly what is being said without presumption, assumption or error.

My interpretation of N.O.I.S.E. stands for:

- N – Negative expectations
- O – Obstinate beliefs
- I – Individual image (self-worth)
- S – Stressed or scared state
- E – Experiences in the past

To start with, you need to understand that the N.O.I.S.E. in the customer's head may distort your natural conversation and make it harder for you to relax and have that nice chat. Being aware of the customer's noise means you can watch out for it, understand it and counter it, just as you would a friend who was distracted or wasn't paying attention when you were talking to them.

First, using my own formula and an NLP communications model, let me explain what the noise consists of. Then we will look at my formula to help you identify and counter the distortion the noise generates in the customer's mind.

All encounters are subject to noise as a distortion of communication. That is because we do not come to an encounter completely free of ourselves or past experience.

Noise is made up of previous experience, especially if it was negative and triggered feelings of guilt, fear or resentment. For example, the last time a salesperson spoke to your customer they were rude and bullying; so the subconscious noise is the expectation that this encounter may be the same.

In addition, the noise is made up of that person's set of personal beliefs and self-worth. So, if a belief is **'all salesmen are liars'**, that will distort the message you are trying to project. If the self-worth suggests, **'I am weak'**, that will colour how the customer feels and perceives the conversation.

The noise is made up of perceptions and assumptions, not truth, so you have to be aware of the possibility of these negative perceptions and assumptions colouring how you are heard. Once you are aware of these potential distortions, as we shall see, it is easy to counter them using the G.R.O.W.T.H.S. U.P.

model in a natural relaxed way.

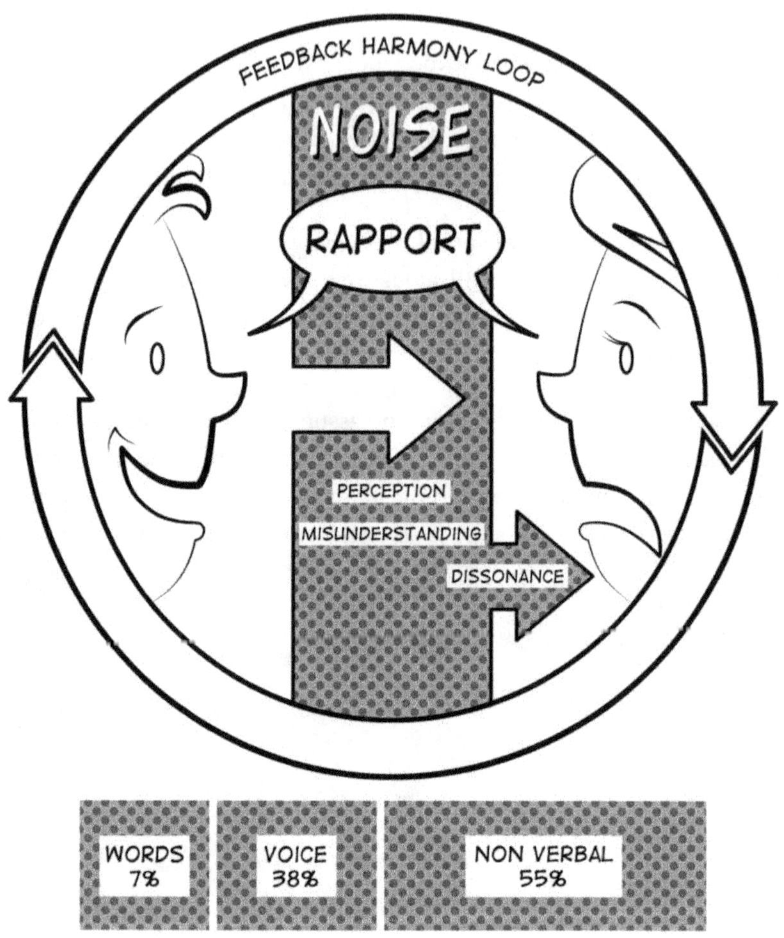

Another view of what I call N.O.I.S.E. is the NLP model, which considers that we filter information by Distorting, Deleting or Generalising how we see the world as in the diagram below.

The filters we use according to NLP are our Values, Beliefs, Attitudes, Memories and Decisions.

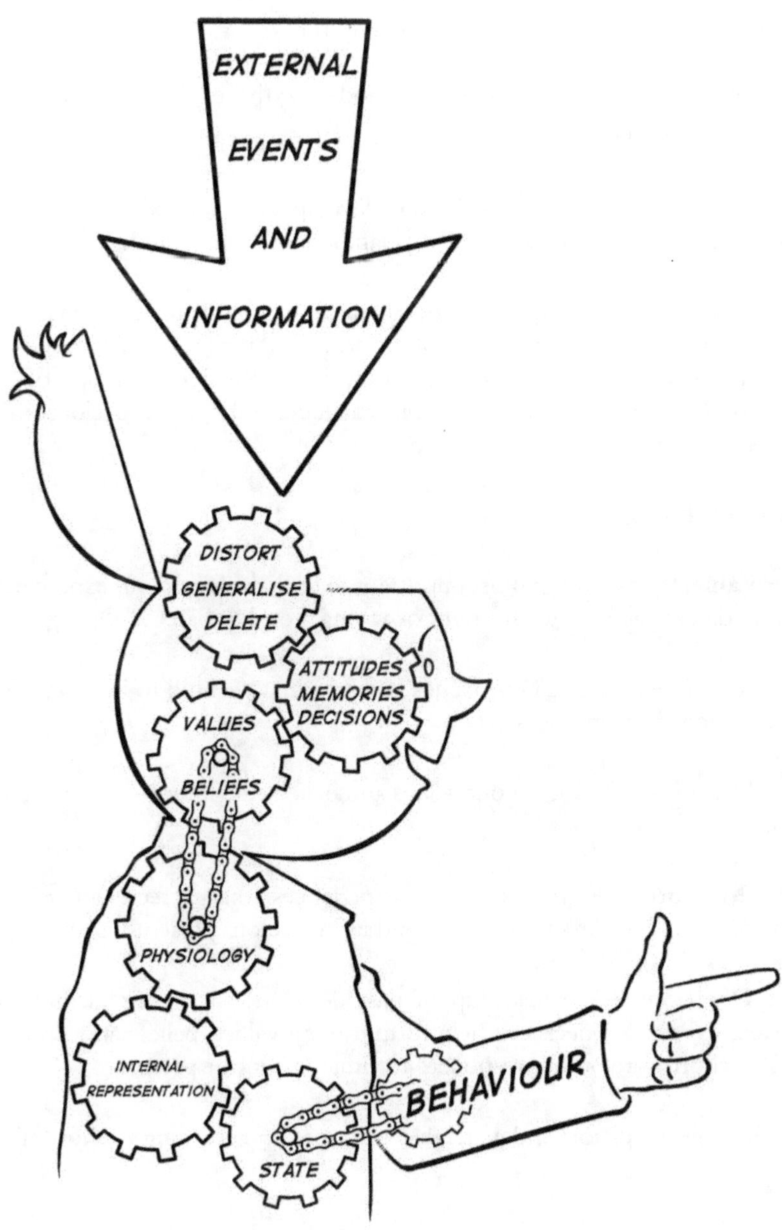

This affects how we see the world and our subsequent behaviour.

Knowledge of this N.O.I.S.E. and the NLP model help us be aware of what affects our customer and our natural conversation and allows us to communicate in a clearer more relaxed and focused way.

To give a bit more detail on the NLP model for those of you who have not come across it before:

The NLP Communication Model was developed by Wyatt Woodsmall and Tad James from the work of Richard Bandler and John Grinder.

We all have to absorb and process vast amounts of information through our senses: up to four million bits of information per second. Consciously assimilating this much information would be impossible, so much of it is processed subconsciously while the remainder that the conscious mind analyses is filtered.

We filter through:

Our Values: those things most important to us, based upon our experiences. Values determine how we see right or wrong, good or bad.

Our Beliefs – flow from our values and are what we hold to be true, about others, the world, and ourselves.

Our Attitudes – flow from our values and beliefs and refer to what we think about specific situations.

Our Memories – are our past experiences that affect our current perceptions. They directly act upon and influence our present behaviours.

Our Decisions – are made up of past decisions about our identity and capability. Previous decisions help form present values, beliefs and attitudes, and exert pressure on our responses to situations in the present.

We then delete, distort and generalise information according to those filters as below.

Deletion – because of the large amount of information that our senses have to cope with and that need to be processed, our brains become selective in where our attention is focused. That focus is based on the most important items at any previous moment in time while other information is deleted from our conscious awareness.

Distortion – the information we receive through our senses is subject to distortion. This is because situations we find difficult, dangerous, unusual or hard to process can be distorted by how we process and interpret that information to conform to our view of reality. Often when we design our future, either as goals or dreams, we distort the potential reality based on current misconceptions.

Generalisation – both positive and negative experiences allow us to learn and make assumptions upon which we base future actions. We apply the general to the specific to shortcut learning and development. Sometimes this works, once touching a fire we learn it burns us and should not be repeated. Sometimes it leads us down false alleys. We are insulted by someone of a particular race or gender and then generalise all people like that are rude.

So as a process, our thoughts are created by information filtered through our senses. These thoughts come together to provide a map of how we see reality. This reality, both sensory and emotional, governs our behaviour. So our reality, in truth, is what we perceive, not what is.

Understanding that everyone's noise exists and everyone's perception is individual based on how they filter reality helps us in our natural conversation to treat our customers as individuals and respond to them accordingly in a focused, positive and relaxed manner.

In summary: 'Knowledge shapes action, focused action ensures positive transactions.'

So now we know what the noise consists of, let's use the formula to understand and counter it.

The first part of the formula is the **<u>"N" for Negative expectations</u>**

Depending on past experience, the customer, before you say a word, may already have negative expectations. Taking into account what we have just looked at let us examine what these might be and how to deal with them.

It might be that the customer has suffered some bad past experiences. For example, the last time they dealt with a salesperson or were buying a product or service, they had a bad experience where the salesperson was rude or unhelpful. This will colour how they expect to be treated this time. That perception is in play before you have even said a word.

They may be the kind of person that listens to and believes gossip, and that has helped them form a generalised negative world view. Remember our filters. An example here might be that by them talking to people and watching the news they are convinced that everyone is out to take advantage of them and that the world is a bad dangerous place. As such they feel they must remain suspicious and closed to protect themselves. And you haven't even said hello yet.

Another factor to take into account is their state of mind when engaging with you. Not everyone will be in a happy, relaxed state like you. Maybe they have come to see you or are talking to you first thing in the morning and they are not morning people; or they are running late because they mislaid their keys. Alternatively, it might be in the afternoon or evening and they have had a stressful day and are not focused on you or the encounter, but rather just thinking about getting home to a hot bath. Being aware of their state will help you deal with it and have that focused, relaxed conversation. Ignorance of it, treating everyone the same, as some salespeople do, will just exacerbate their disconnect and lead to failure rather than success.

The customer's perceptions and interaction with you will also be affected by any physical or physiological problems they may be experiencing: However positive your message and relaxed your conversation, if they are suffering from chronic pain, or even just a headache or are worried about a family situation it will be difficult for them to focus on your message, your N.I.C.E. C.H.A.T.

Finally, the last perception or filter cause you might wish to take into account is any negative environmental aspects that exist at the time of your conversation and exchange. Just imagine that your customer is late for your appointment or running late because of a traffic jam or train strike or delay. They will be frustrated, uptight and irritated; not a good place to start a relaxed, positive conversation. Or it might be that the weather is too hot: it's hard to be relaxed when you are sweating and thirsty or maybe just suffering from a lack of sleep.

So, these are the negative expectations that you might have to counter before you can engage in your positive, relaxed, natural conversation. Now you aware of their existence, what is the solution?

In the diagrams and concepts below, knowledge is power – power to change a negative to a positive. As long as you are aware of the signs that your customer can be distracted by negative expectations, then you can, in a natural way, during your conversation, address these negative expectations so that what you say reinforces a positive view rather than a negative one. Recognise their concerns and rather than ignore them or steamroller over them. Acknowledge them and work with them, turning the negative concern into a positive one by building rapport, treating the customer's state and concern as real, and helping them respectfully work with it by taking them from a dark, negative valley to a sunny upland.

Acknowledgement, sympathy and openness are the tools to help the customer to a better place and allow the natural conversation to develop.

What we are looking at here is to build rapport through our G.R.O.W.T.H.S. U.P.

model and the natural conversation it creates. The rapport, the natural conversation, when linked to the knowledge and awareness you now and will have, helps us to break through the noise and challenge any negative perceptions to create a natural, effective, dialogue which can lead to an exchange and revenue-enhancing transaction.,

To counter the negative and work with our customer's perception and build that rapport it is worth knowing how that perception is broken down as in this model.

(Aka Servqual, as used in my communications workshops)

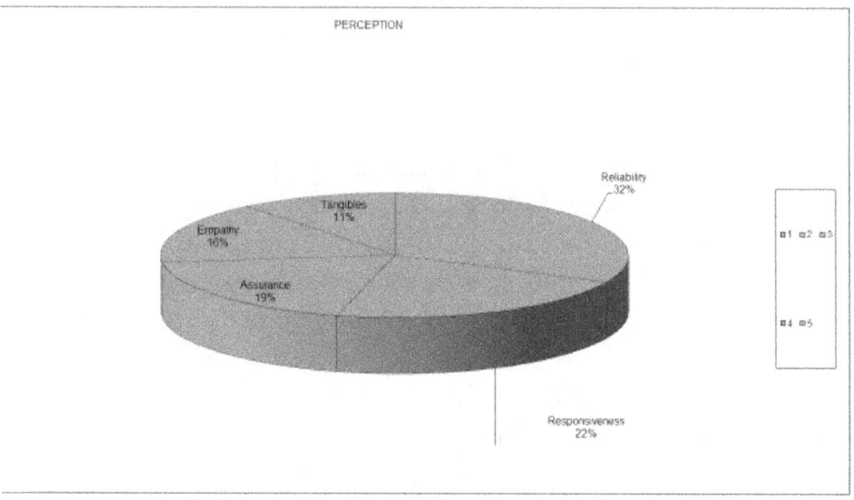

In other words, a customer's perception, made up of their filters, will cause them to ask themselves in a business situation the following, which we must address to build that rapport and have that natural conversation. The customer will be thinking:

- So can I trust you?
- Can I believe what you tell me?
- Will you help me when I need it?
- Do you really care about me?
- Have you got the basics right?
- Does it feel good to do business with you?

Once our natural conversation has addressed these concerns as well as the other negatives we have looked at, it will be easier to break through the N.O.I.S.E. and build the long-term rapport and natural relationship and exchange we want.

We are now aware of perception and the negative aspects of it that we need to break through. To ensure we break through, we also need to be aware of what I call the "Perception Gap". To build the long-term relationship and rapport we must avoid this perception gap. To do that we have to be congruent in what we say and do and be aware of our customer's concerns. The diagram below illustrates this.

AVOIDING PERCEPTION GAPS

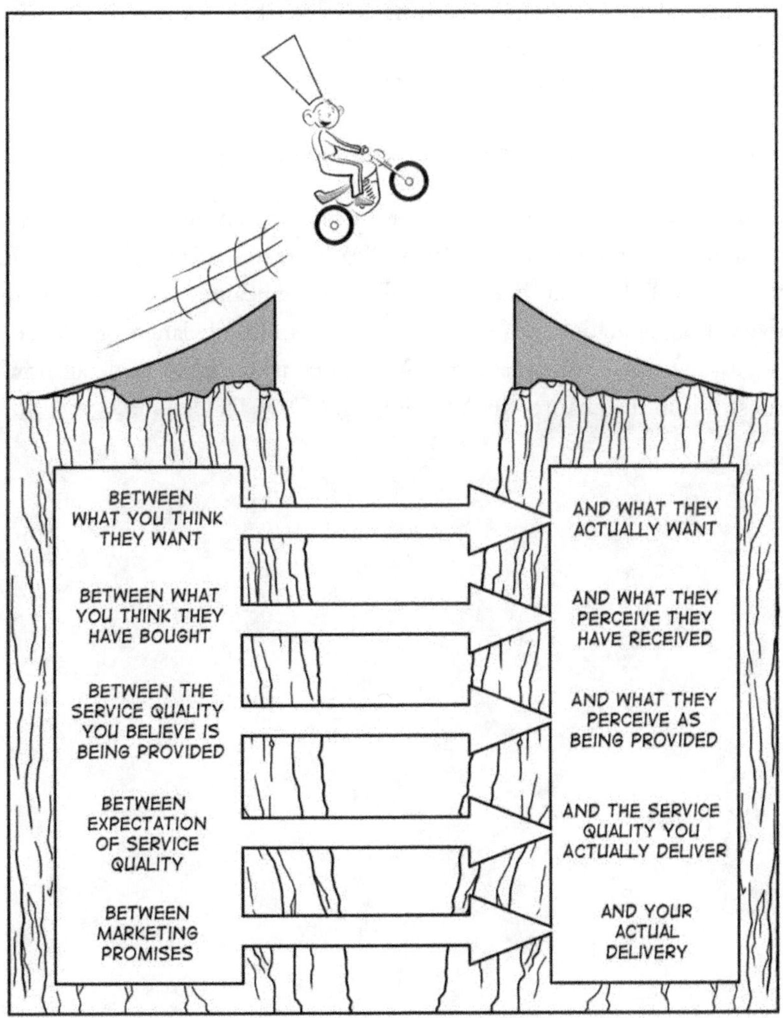

Building a relationship as opposed to just trying to close a sale requires us to be aware of and avoid these gaps. Otherwise the customer will feel short changed and their concept of worth, service and a good transaction will be devalued.

As in old sales techniques, you might close the immediate sale but the perception gap will ensure you get no more from that customer or, as is most likely, all the friends and acquaintances they tell. Bad service perception gaps are communicated fast and far. Dissatisfaction is something we all like to tell others about and with social media making this so easy, if you don't mind the gap you could be sabotaging your business without even knowing it. So, build the rapport, have the natural conversation, deliver what the customer needs and you will assure G.R.O.W.T.H.S. U.P.

For more customers and revenue – Just Mind the Gap

The following diagrams illustrate the noise factors that can affect the creation of rapport and the long-term relationship it creates. It introduces the fact, which we will look at later, that all communication, even our natural conversation, is made up of our words, voice and body language. These are divided as shown in the diagrams. We will consider in more detail how to harness this in the chapter on Applying G.R.O.W.T.H.S. U.P.

COMMUNICATIONS MODEL
VOICE 38%
WORDS 7%
BODY LANGUAGE 55%

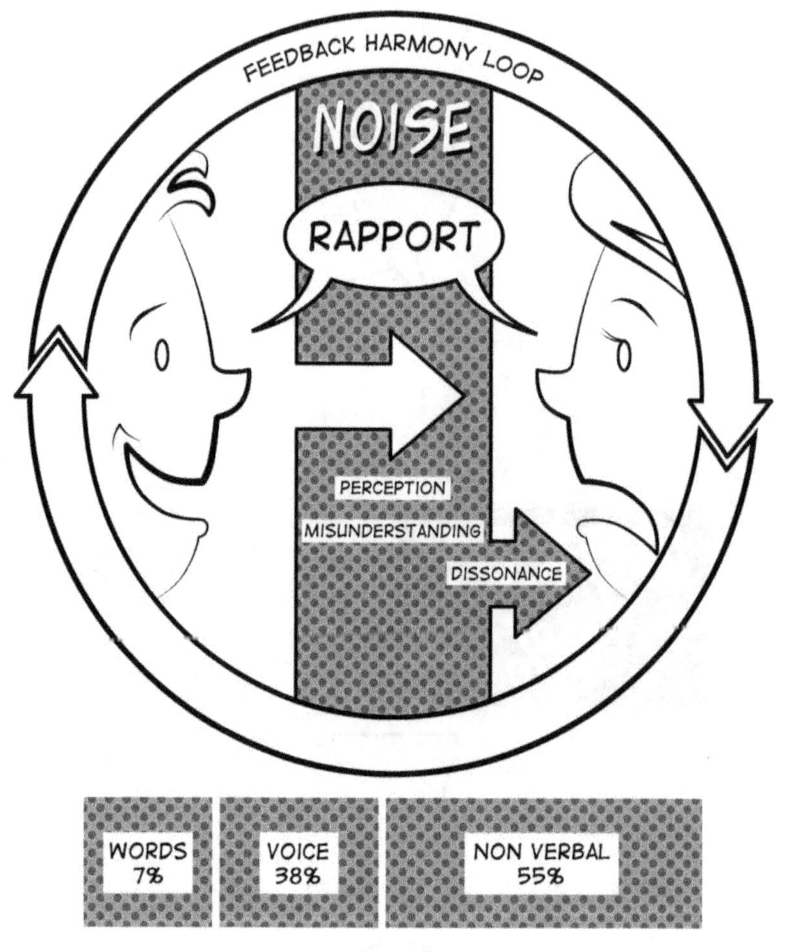

<u>We now turn to the second part of the formula, which concerns the "O" in noise and stands for "Obstinate beliefs".</u>

Everyone you talk to has a set of beliefs they live their life by and which informs their values and world view. As we have seen, this is one of our filters according to the NLP communications model we considered before. Though beliefs can be changed, some are well-embedded and difficult to challenge, and these obstinate beliefs will affect how your customer hears and sees you.

The obstinate beliefs are often reinforced by the filter of generalisations based on a person's limited experience and for our purpose could include the following:

The customer has had several bad experiences with salespeople trying, as they feel, to take advantage of them. The result is that because they feel cheated and fearful after these encounters they come to you with the belief that, in fact, 'all salesmen are con artists.' This can often be linked to the belief that as such 'all salesmen try to rip you off.' Note that this belief has become associated with "All" salesmen, not just some. So this obstinate belief means that when you begin your natural conversation, the filter of noise that will distort how they hear what you say will be biased because of these beliefs. As long as you detect them, then you can counter them and proceed to a more positive environment within which to have your N.I.C.E. C.H.A.T. and relaxed exchange.

The last two obstinate beliefs that may affect your customer and how they perceive you are those based on their experience, or even just the experience of friends. They might believe that people are not honest and as such, because they also see themselves as weak, fear they will be taken advantage of. These beliefs will colour how they regard you and what they hear. Awareness will help you cut through that Noise and enable you to have the positive, relaxed conversation that will make the customer feel happy and safe and allow you to offer your positive message and describe how you can serve their needs and wants.

This diagram gives some ideas of the distortion the noise of beliefs and negativity can create

NOISE DISTORTION OF WHAT YOU SAY AND WHAT YOUR CUSTOMER HEARS IF IN A NEGATIVE STATE ETC.

WHAT YOU SAY	*NOISE* PERCEPTION MISUNDERSTANDING	*WHAT THEY HEAR IF IN A NEGATIVE STATE OR HAVE OBSTINATE BELIEFS ETC*
GOOD MORNING		WHAT'S GOOD ABOUT IT ?
A LOVELY DAY		NOT FOR ME
WHICH COLOUR DO YOU MOST LIKE ?		WHAT'S IT TO YOU ?
WE HAVE THAT ON SPECIAL OFFER		OH A RIP OFF PRICE
WHAT ELSE MIGHT YOU BE LOOKING FOR ?		TRYING TO SELL MORE OF WHAT I DON'T WANT
WHEN WOULD YOU LIKE IT DELIVERED ?		WHY ARE YOU PUSHING ME ?

The solution to countering and circumventing these obstinate beliefs is again understanding and being aware of their possible existence. Their existence can be spotted by your customer's Voice, tone and body language. The way they walk into your shop; the tone they use on the phone, the abruptness of an email exchange or social media messaging: all are indicators of their state negative or positive. This knowledge will help you initiate a relaxed, natural conversation that will not confront these beliefs but gently guide your customer away from any blocks and towards a more relaxed, natural flow. This can lead to an exchange that is mutually beneficial and much more relaxing. If you know they are there and are alert for them, it is much easier, once identified, to gently steer the conversation to the positive and away from the blocks these beliefs might represent.

We now turn to the third part of the formula. This is an important one and refers to the "I", which concerns a person's Individual image and their perception of their self-worth.

One of the things to be aware of, just as you would do when talking to a friend, and as we have seen, is that how someone perceives them self affects how they interpret what you say. We have already looked at filters and the different ways perception is constructed. Now we are going to extend this understanding of perception to include, in more detail, how a person's self-image or self-worth affects how they will react to you.

There are several factors in how people view themselves and their value or self- worth: each needs to be treated differently.

The first type of individual image is what we call the high self-worth individual: This is someone who is confident and relaxed in themselves and will hear and react well to positive messages. They do not feel threatened or intimidated and enjoy and respond well to a naturally relaxed chat.

The approach to use with these individuals is to: use your relaxed, natural manner, which they will happily embrace. Your discussion, choices and options will engage smoothly with them, making the conversation easy. The N.I.C.E. C.H.A.T. will flow naturally to a positive conclusion.

In contrast to this type we have the low self-worth individual. This is someone who may feel intimidated and fearful of your normal natural chat and be resistant to suggestions and options. They may be less assertive and therefore may not feel comfortable communicating. They may feel shy about saying how they really feel or read negative sub-texts into your message.

The approach to use with this kind of person is a gentle, slower, open and consultative type of dialogue, which will result in a better, more natural flow and an improved exchange. A longer time frame should be used to set the scene, which will allow you the opportunity to engage in supportive, less direct dialogue to help them be relaxed and at ease.

In addition to self-worth, there are also externally and internally referenced individuals to consider. Whether they are high or low self-worth, they can be either externally or internally referenced. Different approaches are needed for each.

Externally referenced individuals base self-worth on the need for the approval of others, which can cause them to surrender control. They outsource responsibility for their identity and emotional well-being to other people, needing others to think the best of them and validate their choices and existence. Externally referenced individuals have to consistently seek the approval of others because without it there's no sense of self to maintain them, no inner core of worth. Relying on external validation can be power sapping. Without an internal source they rely on external approval, which can greatly increase their fragility.

The approach here is that when talking to such people it is important to validate their choices as much as possible and if necessary engage and involve their family, colleagues or friends. This will help them feel comfortable with the options and choices that the relaxed, natural N.I.C.E. C.H.A.T. offers them. If you build in such external validation, including endorsements and recommendations, then you will find the exchange goes smoothly; the conversation is relaxed and the result is positive.

For internally referenced individuals you need to understand that they reference their decision-making process and choices on how they feel within themselves. This referencing is from the core of their being and not from some outside source. This means, that ultimately the source of esteem and satisfaction comes from within. Internally referenced individuals believe in their own intrinsic value regardless of how others see them.

Your approach here is that your natural conversation should focus on them and on what they are interested in and what helps them make their choices. They want facts they can consider, not outside referencing or endorsements.

<u>The next part of the formula we need to look at is the "S" which refers to our customer's potentially "Stressed or scared state".</u>

It is important, just as you would be when talking to a friend, to be aware if the person you are communicating with is troubled, stressed or scared. If they are not in a good place psychologically, then it will be harder to have a natural conversation and discuss all the positive outcomes and choices available, as people in a negative state find it extremely hard to focus on positive messages. We have previously looked at some of the factors that would cause your customer to be in that stressed or scared state. They might be caused by environmental, personal, physical or psychological events. These may well affect their perception, judgement and actions.

Stressed or scared customers may be preoccupied by personal concerns and not as receptive to the message as if they were not stressed. Customers who are angry about something external before you even have your discussion will have their N.O.I.S.E. turned up high; a psychological barrier to communication that might cause them to misinterpret what you are saying. Indeed, stressed or scared customers are not only in a psychologically bad place, but are also in a physiologically difficult state.

When someone is suffering from stress, anxiety or fear there is a physical reaction that will affect how they are and how they think and act. Knowing this will help you deal with it effectively.

When you are stressed, adrenaline and cortisol flood your body. These chemicals are designed to prepare the body for what is known as the fight flight or freeze response. That is, their body's metabolism speeds up, the heart beats faster, blood pressure increases (which is why some people suffer from headaches when they get stressed) and their body goes into overdrive. That is all very well in small bursts, but over time it wears the body down. These chemicals also, by the way, suppress the immune system; so stressed people leave themselves open to a greater risk of illness.

At the same time, if you think back to when you may have been stressed or uptight – maybe in your car stuck in a traffic jam or on a crowded, delayed train, you know what pushes your buttons. But here's the thing; remember how your body reacted. Were your hands clenched, shoulders taught, neck muscles tight, your stomach in knots? All of these are common physical manifestations of stress; and as I am sure you can realise, keeping those muscles under tension is bad for the body, burns energy unnecessarily and can lead to headaches and muscle pain. These are signs of stress you can look for in your customer as clues to how they are feeling. Knowing and being aware of how they are and what they are enduring will help you deal with it better.

The approach for stressed or scared customers who are anxious or fearful is to spend time at the beginning of the conversation talking about relaxed non-relevant subjects that will help you and them focus on a positive emotional and mental environment. This will help distract and remove them from the stressed or angry state they were in to begin with – ***a bit like offering a virtual cup of tea.*** When their state is more relaxed, then your normal, natural conversation, your N.I.C.E. C.H.A.T., can continue with a receptive relaxed customer and help ensure a positive exchange and good outcome.

If you have a chance to offer them a seat or indeed a cup of tea or a glass of water, this can help, as can calming music and lighting, though this is a subject in its own right. We will look more at the environment and how to maximise it for G.R.O.W.T.H.S. U.P. in the chapter on your Conversational environment.

Finally we end this review of breaking through the N.O.I.S.E. by looking at the last letter in the formula, the "E" which stands for our "Experiences in the past".

In every conversation you have, whether with a friend, relative, colleague or customer, you should know that one element of the N.O.I.S.E. that distorts the message you give, the dialogue you have, is the experience that person has had in their past up to and including the moment you enter into your natural conversation.

We cannot ignore or forget our past and what happened then colours how we see the present. Whether we react positively or negatively to past experiences, they will shape how we perceive the present. This letter is to remind us of all we have looked at so far in N.O.I.S.E. – the negative expectations, obstinate beliefs, image and self-worth, the stressed and scared state. All of this potential baggage has been formed in the past, as we have seen, but will affect our perceptions and actions in the present.

Though we are operating in the now – and the G.R.O.W.T.H.S. U.P. model works to help us talk, work and focus on the present – we must always be aware of the experiences in the past that our customer, and indeed ourselves, have brought to the conversation and exchange.

The following quotes sum up that relationship for me.

'Awareness as always brings the present to life and that knowledge creates positive results.'

'The past is a mirror which reflects on our mind the present.'

'Your past is always your past. Even if you forget it, it remembers you. Sarah Dessen, *What Happened to Goodbye*

The approach to take has been discussed before. Suffice it to say, that in any conversation, look for indicators that the topic under discussion resonates in either a positive or negative way with your customer. If it appears there was a positive past experience, amplify and validate it. If a negative one, acknowledge then isolate and exclude it by gently steering the conversation to safer, more positive topics.

In conclusion, breaking through and dealing with N.O.I.S.E. is not as complex or as daunting as it may first seem. All you need is to be sensitive and aware, just as you would be when talking to a friend, in a relaxed way, knowing that there are factors that will affect how they hear and see you.

Once you are sensitive to the existence of N.O.I.S.E., and conduct your relaxed conversation, tuned in to your customer and being focused on them in the present, in the now, you will pick up all the necessary clues. With practice you will automatically adjust your natural speech rhythms and conversation to relax, reassure and engage with your customer leading to a natural exchange and positive result.

10 YOU NEED TO STAY ON THE RIGHT PA.T.H.

We have learnt how to S.M.I.L.E., have a N.I.C.E. C.H.A.T. and break through the N.O.I.S.E. It is now time to amplify our skills and link them to our greater awareness by continuing to develop how to apply the G.R.O.W.T.H.S. U.P. model. In this chapter we are going to learn how to say on the right PA.T.H.

PA.T.H. stands for:

- P A – PAint a picture
- T – Tell a story
- H – Have a conversation

In your NICE CHATS, your natural conversation, there is a smooth, easy path to a natural flow and successful exchange and a mutually agreeable outcome that avoids the rocky path of sales, manipulation, stress and confusion

In this section I want to give you some ideas in how to make that PA.T.H. as smooth as possible.

You may have heard of another of the NLP concepts; of people having a dominant way of thinking and using language. It is known as VAK and stands for Visual, Auditory or Kinaesthetic. By engaging in the right way, in your natural conversation, with language that reflects how your customer thinks, you will find the natural flow better and more relaxed. To help this process you can use these concepts while you Paint a picture, Tell a story and Have a conversation. This mix of methods and ways of talking will help you improve the natural flow of your conversation and improve the engagement and outcome of your discussion.

Below you will find and overview of NLP and VAK (Please skip this section if these terms are familiar to you).

NLP

The best definition I have found is from one of the founders of NLP, Robert Dilts, and I reproduce that here from his website:

NLP stands for ***Neuro-Linguistic Programming,*** *a name that encompasses the three most influential components involved in producing human experience: neurology, language and programming. The neurological system regulates how our bodies function, language determines how we interface and communicate with other people and our programming determines the kinds of models of the world we create. Neuro-Linguistic Programming describes the fundamental dynamics between mind (neuro) and language (linguistic) and how their interplay affects our body and behaviour (programming).*

NLP is a ***pragmatic school of thought*** *- an 'epistemology' - that addresses the many levels involved in being human. NLP is a multi-dimensional process that involves the development of behavioral competence and flexibility, but also involves strategic thinking and an understanding of the mental and cognitive processes behind behavior. NLP provides tools and skills for the development of states of individual excellence, but it also establishes a system of empowering beliefs and presuppositions about what human beings are, what communication is and what the process of change is all about. At another level, NLP is about self-discovery, exploring identity and mission. It also provides a framework for understanding and relating to the 'spiritual' part of human experience that reaches beyond us as individuals to our family, community and global systems. NLP is not only about competence and excellence, it is about wisdom and vision.*

Robert Dilts Find out more from his website http://www.robertdilts.com/

Now we have defined NLP, let us look at one of its constructs. The Visual, Auditory and Kinaesthetic (VAK) model was utilised by Fleming in 2001. This model suggests most people have a dominant or preferred style of learning. Some, however, mix and blended two or three styles. The balance of the blend is individual. These three styles consist of visual, auditory and kinaesthetic learners: I refer to them in my PA.T.H. model here as Visual, Auditory and Kinaesthetic Acquirers.

If we start with the Visual Acquirers, to engage effectively with them it is important to know that generally they**:** access information through seeing and thinking in pictures. They need to create vivid mental images to retain information and so enjoy looking at maps, charts, pictures, videos and movies.

They have visual skills that are often demonstrated in puzzle building, reading, writing and understanding charts and graphs. They generally have a good sense of direction and enjoy sketching and painting while creating visual metaphors and analogies. They excel at manipulating and interpreting images as well as constructing, fixing and designing practical objects.

On the other hand, Auditory Acquirers generally: access information through listening and have highly developed auditory skills. They are often good at speaking and presenting and think in words rather than pictures. They learn best through verbal lectures, discussions, talking things through and listening to what others have to say.

They demonstrate their skills in listening very carefully, speaking accurately and writing creatively. They stand out as excellent storytellers, explaining, teaching and using humour effectively. They generally find it easier understanding the syntax and meaning of words, remembering information, arguing their point of view, and analysing language usage.

Meanwhile, Kinaesthetic Acquirers generally: develop and communicate through moving, doing and touching. They express themselves through movement and have good sense of balance and eye-hand coordination. They also remember and process information through interacting with the space around them. Part of this type of acquisition means that they find it hard to sit still for long periods and may become distracted by their need for activity and exploration.

In addition, they demonstrate skills in physical coordination, athletic ability and hands-on experimentation. They are sensitive to body language and engage in acting and miming. They are adept at using their hands to create or build. They love dancing and expressing emotions through the use of their body.

So with that overview in our mind let us now focus on staying on the smooth PA.T.H. To do that we first have to know how to apply the PA in PA.T.H.; in other words, how to **Paint a picture.**

Referring to our Visual Acquirers: as you can see, Painting a picture as you talk to them will resonate closely with their way of acquiring information and help you have a more flowing, natural conversation. Using words to paint a picture and set a scene will help your customer **See** what they need and how you can help them acquire it.

In painting your picture use words such as: can you **Imagine;** taking a long term **View**; seeing something from many **Viewpoints;** seeing **Clearly**. Use visual aids to paint your picture, as this is useful for this group. So if you have pictures of your products or a PowerPoint demonstration, Visual acquirers will respond favourably to this. Your natural conversation can paint a picture, which will help them better **See** what they need.

On the other hand, if you have someone who is an Auditory Acquirer you can still Paint your picture. Here, words are even more your ally, as Auditory Acquirers prefer to absorb information through words. So, pick your words carefully and precisely; use detail to paint the picture of your product and service. Words such as: **I hear what you say; that is music to my ears; we are singing from the same hymn sheet; that sounds right to me; that screams out for a**… Remember to describe your product or service in detail. You might say your product **Speaks for itself** so if you could **put in a Good Word for it**…

Finally, Kinaesthetic Acquirers: as this group prefers the physical touching and interaction with objects and space, you can Paint a picture by engaging with them both in a natural conversation and also in the physical environment. If you have a product they can feel, touch, smell or taste, then use this to paint your picture. If you provide a service, use props such as papers or books, or some physical example to paint a picture for them. For instance, if your service was training and you wanted to illustrate how you appealed to the subconscious mind, you could use a physical toy of an iceberg or pyramid to illustrate this example.

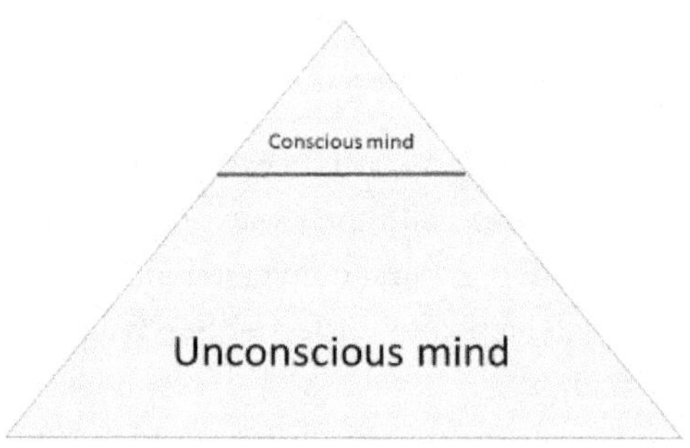

Use words such as: **Grasp** or **Clutch, Gut feeling, Embedded, Getting round barriers** or **Hard hitting**. Tell a **Gripping tale** where you can: **Remove barriers** and **Hammer out a solution**. **Plant a seed** and get to the **Root of the problem.** These words, along with physical interaction with their environment, will help you have a natural conversation with Kinaesthetic Acquirers and help you paint a picture which grips them.

So there we are, we have Painted a picture and are now on our smooth path to success.

Now we must look at the "T" in PA.T.H., which is all about how to Tell a story.

To help you even further to have a relaxed, natural conversation that will help you make sure your G.R.O.W.T.H.S. U.P. we need now to use one of the most natural of all human skills, one that will bind your customer to you and engage their interest; allowing your conversation to flow and to ensure your success. To stay on the PA.T.H., you now need to Tell a story.

Storytelling is one of the oldest human skills and we all love a good story. Most of us are brought up on stories when, as children, our parents would read us bedtime stories or we would hear teachers or friends telling stories. Stories, if told naturally and honestly, engage the listener and personalise you and a product or service that might seem to the customer cold or distant.

Storytelling also stimulates a powerful neurological response. According to neuroeconomist Paul Zak, research suggests our brains produce the stress hormone cortisol, which we have already identified, during tense moments in a story. This allows us to pay attention and focus, while a part of the story that has sweet or gentle parts to it stimulates the release of oxytocin, the chemical that promotes positive feelings of connection and empathy. Other neurological research indicates that a happy ending causes the limbic part of the brain to release dopamine, the hormone that awakens feelings of optimism and hope.

So stories chemically and psychologically spark emotions. They stimulate our emotional side, the part that deals with intuition, as opposed to the rational part of our brain. It allows us to connect emotionally with our customers and build that rapport by engaging with that side of their character. Logic doesn't build rapport, emotion does and storytelling will greatly speed up that process.

Telling your customer a story also helps to put things in context and explain a maybe complex product, service or situation in a more meaningful light.

Stories work because they hark back to a more primitive time. They link us to the time of legends and myth, of fairy tales and heroes. As such they have a powerful effect on us at many levels and in many ways. They should not be underestimated in their power and effect.

We are conditioned to think emotionally in metaphor and analogy. Stories bring that together in a frame of reference that is meaningful, understandable and engaging. This makes the message and connection stronger and more permanent than normal dialogue or conversation. Our storytelling taps into the imagination; it creates our customer's shared experience with us, and helps us build the rapport, provide clarity and bond with their needs and desires. Stories engage the listener in the narrative, offering a more powerful method of communication and understanding than a mere logical, left brain discussion.

So, use your own vast knowledge and experience or information and stories that you have heard from others. We have all had similar experiences so with practice it is not difficult to naturally weave a relevant, honest, congruent, story into you conversation.

By using phrases that genuinely link your experience to those of the customer, telling a story will allow a relaxed, natural flow. Phrases such as 'That reminds me of…', 'I remember when…', or 'Imagine if, you will, a situation when I was…'. Before the punchline, remember to ask the customer if they can imagine what happened next rather than telling them. This will engage their imagination and allow you to enhance both your and their experience of your fun and enjoyment. If they guess correctly, they have bought into your product or service. If they guess incorrectly, it gives you a chance to explain the product or service ending to the story in more detail; a Win-Win.

Storytelling is a natural and powerful tool to help you stay on your smooth PA.T.H. to making sure your G.R.OW.T.H.S. U.P.

Finally to complete our smooth PA.T[H] we need to bring this all together by doing what we do naturally: **<u>Examining the "H" which stands for Having a conversation.</u>**

This highlights that all we have looked at from SMILE to a NICE CHAT and breaking through the NOISE, is all about having a naturally relaxed conversation, not using static formulas or scripts. The tools we have looked at so far are to help you be in the moment and give you, with practice, subconscious awareness so that you can have that natural, relaxed conversation.

Adam Grant, in his book *Give and Take*, highlights the fact that in selling the most successful are those who are givers not takers, i.e., those who ask questions and allow the customers the joy of talking. The mindset is not to sell but help as Grant states on pg 136: 'a Givers defining quality is asking questions which is a form of powerless communication and an effective sales technique.'

My take on this is the old saying that we have one mouth and two ears, so we should listen twice as much as we talk in a conversation. Having a conversation is exactly that; it is a dialogue full of questions and interaction. Monologues and sales scripts do not treat the customer as an individual or find out their true need. The G.R.O.W.T.H.S. U.P. model of a N.I.C.E. C.H.A.T., a natural conversation, promotes an individual approach where caring for and serving the customer's needs is made easy by that relaxed dialogue, that natural interplay. Having a conversation gently, respectfully and with fun and humour, will generate revenue and more customers, both in the present and in the future, more than any manipulative sales technique or set-in-stone process ever will.

Internalise the ideas, practice relaxing into a natural conversation, and you can be sure you will feel good, your customers will feel relaxed and you will make sure your G.R.O.W.T.H.S. U.P. By satisfying yourself and your customers you will create a Win-Win exchange and revenue enhanced transaction.

All you have to do is have that relaxed conversation and the rest will naturally follow; if not every time, then enough that you will ensure your G.R.O.W.T.H.S. U.P.

The conversation is similar to that you have with close friends. It is calm; you and your customer are aligned, so there are no hesitant pauses or awkward silences. That is because 'Energy flows where attention goes' and your conversation is positive, energised and focused, leading to that positive conclusion.

So staying on the right PA.T.H.; painting a picture, telling a story and having that conversation, will allow you to utilise the G.R.O.W.T.H.S. U.P. model. Combining your S.M.I.L.E. and N.I.C.E. C.H.A.T. while having broken through the N.O.I.S.E., your PA.T.H. to success is assured. Next, we will give you even more tools to help you utilise the G.R.O.W.T.H.S. U.P. model to its maximum and generate more customers and the extra revenue you deserve and need.

11 UTILISING FCO$^{2®}$ FOR G.R.O.W.T.H.S. U.P.

FCO^2 was the subject of my first book and is a formula that stands for Focus, Congruence and Control. In this chapter the formula is targeted specifically at making your G.R.O.W.T.H.S. U.P. model work more effectively and help you generate that extra revenue and increased customer base even more easily. This is achieved by providing you with added resources to help you operate the model, thus placing you in the right frame to be even more successful.

For a more in-depth view on how FCO^2 can affect your whole life for the better, not just how it can be utilised to improve G.R.O.W.T.H.S. U.P., please see my first book *FCO^2. The ultimate formula for a happy life.* (available from Amazon).

How this FCO^2 Formula applies to G.R.OW.T.H.S. U.P is as follows:

"**F" stands for Focus** and in this context means realising that G.R.OW.T.H.S. U.P. is the best way for you to gain revenue and customers. To make the model work effectively and speedily it is recommended you focus completely on practicing, internalising and applying this natural technique. By focusing on the model and its resources and by practicing the methods, they will become unconscious competencies that are natural and easy to use even for the most shy and introverted of you.

Focus will help you go from unconscious incompetence to unconscious competence where, completely naturally, you will have flowing, relaxed conversations that will achieve G.R.OW.T.H.S. U.P. This progression from unconscious incompetence to unconscious competence refers to Maslow's Four Stages of Learning as seen here.

Unconscious Incompetence
You don't know that you don't know how to do something
Conscious Incompetence
You know that you don't know how to do something and it bothers you
Conscious Competence
You know that you know how to do something and it takes effort
Unconscious Competence
You know how to do something and it's second nature

The first part of the formula, Focus, has five elements, each one of which we will look at in more detail.

- Element 1) is the need to identify a clear goal.
- Element 2) is Clarifying a clear path to achieve the goal.
- Element 3) is Deciding on the resources needed to achieve that goal then.
- Element 4) is Taking the first step and finally.
- Element 5) is Sticking to the journey, ignoring the roadblocks, Focusing on the NOW till your goal is achieved.

So let us look at each of these five elements individually and see how they apply directly in helping you ensure more of your G.R.OW.T.H.S. U.P.

Element 1) is the need to identify a clear goal.

First, it must be a goal you truly want to achieve for yourself: not a goal others want you to go for or are pushing you to attain. So you must believe that G.R.OW.T.H.S. U.P. is a process and a project that you can devote time and energy to because it will help you grow your business naturally and that is something you really want.

For example: I knew a parent who always wanted to be a professional footballer and never quite made it. He pushed his son all through his early years and teens to practice, play, and try out for the local team. The problem was his son hated football and wanted to be a musician. For twelve years he forced himself to obey his father till finally a team rejected him. He had a case of depression and it was only during this phase of his life that through a series of events he was finally able to talk to his father about what **he** wanted. His father had never realised his son's true desire. It was only after they had these discussions that the father realised his son's real goals and that the son was able to pursue his true goal. His depression lifted and now he is a successful musician. There are many such examples.

You must identify **your** clear goal that is right for **you**. So, be honest that this goal is your goal.

If you are still having trouble deciding on growing your business with G.R.OW.T.H.S. U.P. , imagine where you would like to be in one, five and ten years' time. Really imagine where you are at that time, what job you are doing, your personal situation and geographical location. How much more do you want or need to earn for the life you really want now and in the future? Will G.R.OW.T.H.S. U.P. help you attain your goals? If yes, then your Focus is correct and you can continue happy and energised.

Don't second guess it or criticise it intellectually. Think it again, feel it – does it feel right? If it does, without emotional reservation, then it is the right goal for you to pursue.

Element 2) is clarifying a clear path to achieve the goal

This second element of Focus – clarifying a clear path to achieve that goal is easy with G.R.OW.T.H.S. U.P. as we give you the tools to help you on this path. As your goal is clear, it is now necessary to illuminate the path that will lead you to your goal. Now is the time to organise your thoughts and life with the **end** in mind.

Remember your goal, Generating revenue without the hassle, using G.R.OW.T.H.S. U.P. , is the light you must constantly head towards, the tune in your head that always stays with you. Your life is now bound by your goal and how to reach it. Everything that contributes to the path that will let you reach your goal should be embraced; anything that distracts or slows you on your journey or tries to divert you must be ruthlessly put aside.

In this, your inner journey and your outer voyage – for you and you alone – there should be no excuses. Deviation is **not** an option; prevarication or delay should be rejected. If you do find yourself losing focus or becoming distracted then take time to reassess if this goal and this path is really the one you want.

As Confucius said, '**Choose a job you love, and you will never have to work a day in your life**', so too with this focus. If it feels right and becomes easy and second nature then it is for you. If it is fun, relaxing and you look forward to trying and applying it, then embrace it completely. You have found something that you can enjoy, and that will increase revenue and customers for you. If you are struggling or find this model or path difficult or awkward then maybe you should take time away from it and re-consider if it is the model that really works for you. Each person is an individual and each path is unique. If the G.R.OW.T.H.S. U.P. path is for you, welcome to every joyous step. If not, then maybe just take some elements from this journey and use them how and where you can in a positive and energised way. In any event, thank you for joining me on this journey however many steps you take.

To continue...

What elements of G.R.OW.T.H.S. U.P. do you need to consider in order to gain that clarity?

Well, let us consider timescale. How long honestly do you need to achieve your G.R.OW.T.H.S. U.P. goal? What do you need to change, improve or even reject in your life for the path to be clear, uncluttered and free of obstruction and diversion?

This could mean a change of personal, business circumstances or even a physical move. In other words, to achieve your goal of making sure the G.R.OW.T.H.S. U.P. model helps you generate that increased revenue and customers, are you in the right business, in the right location with the right people around you to help you operate the model and reach your goal? These decisions focus you and mean your path is clean and clear and is therefore easier to stick to and embrace.

As an example, a friend of mine decided their goal was to change career to develop skills that they had not used for a long time. To achieve that goal they realised they would need to change job. But when it came to it, fear of rejection, of not being offered another job, or dropping their salary, trapped them into staying where they were. Years later they would be heard to say 'If only.'

Don't you let yourself **Ever** say that. Life only exists in the NOW. Once focused on your true goal, clarify your path and stick to it. Otherwise, instead of being happy and fulfilled, your life will be full of regret and lost opportunity.

'Live in the Now and look forward with positive energy not back with regret.'

Element 3) is Deciding on the resources needed to achieve that goal.

Again, with G.R.OW.T.H.S. U.P. , it is so much easier to know what resources you need as this book and project provide you with a wide range of skills, tools and resources to help you achieve your goal.

In addition to the resources provided in this book you might want to consider some additional personal resources such as: improving your personal fitness, obtaining an extra revenue stream, a vehicle, some new software or hardware, maybe even a business partner, extra or less staff. Whatever the resources you need; however many and varied they may be, list the resources you really need and ensure they are all in place at whatever part of the journey they are required

Think of a film director; they need to plan out all the equipment, cameras and paraphernalia, location, scripts, costumes and props before they can start filming. Otherwise they will be unable to complete their project or shoot their film. You are your own director: make sure you list, manage and use your resources wisely. If you do, you will be able to stick to your clear path and achieve your goal.

Simple resources such as to-do lists and Excel spreadsheets are a cost friendly way to help achieve this. I find that the Microsoft programme One Note is excellent for prioritised to-do lists and Excel great for tracking multiple needs. If you are more ambitious, MS Project or a similar project management software can help organise and structure your journey.

So, there we have it; the first three elements of Focus are completed. The fourth is both simple and sometimes the most difficult.

Element 4) is Taking the first step.

It is said that the longest journey begins with a single step and that is just as true in this journey to reach your goal of ensuring your G.R.OW.T.H.S. U.P. Many people allow their own fears and insecurities to hold them back and block their chance of achieving happiness. It is absolutely essential that once you have identified and committed yourself to your goal of G.R.OW.T.H.S. U.P. , and gathered your resources, that you do indeed take that first vital step.

Too many people plan but are unable to put that plan into action. Your focus, your honesty and belief, will let you take that first step. As long as your goal is clear and honest then you owe it to yourself to walk towards it. Fear of the unknown or change and an inability to move out of our comfort zone can make taking that first step difficult or even impossible for some. Often people prefer to stay where they are even if that situation is bad for them or unprofitable rather than take the risk of trying something new. The future is to be embraced not feared. If you want to change and make things better, as I am sure you do if you are reading this book, then feel the energy that change brings and the excitement of the new adventure.

If not, being stuck will just leave you feeling sad, resentful and de-motivated.

As they say in NLP, **'If you always do what you have always done you always get what you always got.'** Break the cycle, go for it; your future is waiting for you; your G.R.OW.T.H.S. U.P. is ready to generate that extra revenue and customers. Just apply it.

No symphony exists till the first note is played; no journey begins till the first step is taken; no painting till brush touches canvas. So do not hesitate-Apply the old Latin phrase *CARPE DIEM* – Seize the day – Live in the Now – And remember:

'Hope dictates effort and Effort dictates results.'

Element 5) Sticking to the journey, ignoring the roadblocks, Focusing on the NOW till your goal is achieved.

As we have said, you have begun your quest on your road to happiness; your goal is the motorway sign that directs you, the view of the mountain peak that inspires you and the epic piece of music that continues to sound in your head. Keep those signs, images, sounds and feelings always with you: they are your map. In all you do, in every action you take, every word you utter, every feeling you experience, ask yourself one thing and one thing alone. Does this take me closer to my goal, help me achieve what I seek, or will it divert me from my route or mean it takes longer to reach what I am aiming for. If it takes you closer, embrace it without hesitation. If it seeks to divert you, distract you, or delay you, reject it immediately. If you concentrate on the positive, live life in the Now and act always in pursuit of your goal while rejecting diversion, then you will stick to your journey, stay on the right path and reach your goal faster, making your route to happiness stronger, more profound and more worthwhile.

G.R.OW.T.H.S. U.P. will help you to your goal of generating increased revenue and customers without hassle. So, practice, internalise and utilise it and that revenue growth will happen and you will spend the journey feeling happy, energised, positive, good about yourself and relaxed.

We now come to the second part of the FCO² Formula – the first "C" which stands for Congruence.

Congruence is defined as: 'Agreement, harmony or compatibility', something which allows an uninterrupted flow of thought and emotion when in pursuit of a common goal. Congruence is that situation where everything works together, without doubt or obstruction, for a common and clear purpose.

In the context of G.R.OW.T.H.S. U.P. , this means that to achieve your goal of G.R.OW.T.H.S. U.P. , and to maintain your focus and your energy, you will find it far easier if you are Congruent. Congruence will help you maximise your energy flow and help you achieve your goal of G.R.OW.T.H.S. U.P. with less effort, more power and greater well-being.

First it is important to understand that ***being congruent takes no willpower.*** You have heard people say; 'Oh yes, I stuck to the diet through sheer willpower' or 'I finished that race on pure willpower', or even 'You need willpower to stop drinking or smoking.'

If you need willpower to achieve anything then you are not congruent and you are fighting against yourself. You can never win that battle in the long run, which is why so many short-term gains end up as long-term disasters. Think about that as we explore being congruent in more detail.

Physical Congruence

With that mind, let us first look at physical congruence or being congruent in our body. This is the first of two legs that support congruence and your well-being. The second is Psychological congruence, which we will examine later. I wonder what you are imagining now when I tell you that being congruent in your body, physical congruence, is essential for true health and happiness. Being congruent is about harmony; it is a reflection of an uninterrupted flow of energy. Like a river flowing swiftly along its course, or a piece of music played flawlessly without interruption; the energy is free, natural and unforced.

So how does this relate to your body, to the physical? Have you guessed yet? Well there are several elements to your body being congruent. There is food or diet; that is diet with a small "D". Don't worry; this is not another diet fad. Additionally there is exercise, sleep, freedom from stress, and relaxation. For perfect physical congruence all these need to be balanced correctly. Get these elements right and your energy will flow freely and you will be on the way to health and happiness. Get them wrong and you set up for yourself numerous blocks and dams that will interrupt your energy flow and health. That will make it much harder to achieve your goal of generating revenue and gaining more customers in a relaxed, natural way.

Let's look at these elements of physical congruence in some more detail.

Element 1) Food

The first element is Food. This is not a pamphlet on diet; there is enough information available now from many sources to help you decide what you should eat. So let's be honest with each other – forget fad diets. Do you know why they only work, if at all, generally in the short term? Because you need willpower to stay on them. And as we have said, if you need willpower you are fighting against yourself, so you can never win. That's why, whatever your weight, if you have tried diets you have probably tried many. They work for a short time and then your old eating habit reasserts itself. This is because you are not congruent and the incorrect eating pattern is not a problem to be cured, merely a symptom of other areas where you are struggling. Cure those and you will become congruent and eating correctly will no longer be a problem.

You only need to stick to a couple of basic rules where food is concerned to help you be physically congruent.

1) To lose weight or not increase it, energy intake must be less than energy used or expended. In other words, don't eat more calories than you can burn off in day. Adjust how much you eat or how much you exercise so that the equation is either equal, to maintain your weight, or less on your intake, to reduce it. In the end it really is that basic. Anyone **<u>can</u>** do it, so why don't we? It's not the diet, it's the other areas where we are not congruent we need to fix. However, in the meantime, till these are fixed, start to apply the formula I mentioned to help you on your journey to physical congruence.

2) We are what we eat. If you want your body to have energy and keep healthy then it's obvious you need to eat the right food. For a car to run it needs the right fuel, otherwise it performs badly or breaks down. Our bodies are no different. So it really is not rocket science to know that eating fresh fruit, vegetables, lean meats like chicken and fish – and keeping alcohol and drugs like coffee and tea to sensible levels – is only common sense. If you exist on a diet of fast food, pre-prepared meals and junk food then your body will be unable to give you the energy and health you need. You certainly cannot be congruent and you will not be healthy and happy.

That's all there is to the secret of the link between food and being congruent except one last thing. If you are saying to yourself, 'I don't have time or the money to eat healthily', take a moment to check out how long it takes to boil vegetables, grill a piece of chicken or fish or boil or bake a potato. You will find it's cheaper to eat sensibly, takes no more time, and you will be doing yourself a power of good. Try it for a week. If after that you feel less energetic and less positive than before then go back to your old ways. I know you **will** feel better, more positive, more energised. Do what you feel is honestly right for you and you will gain the benefits.

Element 2) Exercise

The second element in being physically congruent is to do with exercise. Exercise and food are related. To be physically congruent your body needs to be maintained. It's like our friend, the car. If you don't turn over the engine regularly or charge the battery then when you do need to use it, it will let you down. It's the same with our bodies. They need exercise so that all the muscles, as well as the heart and brain, are kept in good condition.

Again, I am not saying you need to spend a fortune joining a gym and working out five times a week – unless of course you want to. However you should grab every opportunity to exercise, even if it's walking up stairs instead of using a lift. Maybe you are stuck at a desk at your work most of the day. If so, use any breaks you have to walk, outside, round the office, whatever. Don't just sit there; get your muscles working. Try walking at weekends or maybe cycling, if you enjoy that. If you have the chance to swim or go to the gym as well, that is an added bonus. Whatever you do, whatever your budget or lifestyle, make exercise a natural and welcome part of your day. Establish a routine, even if it's only ten minutes a day, so the exercise allows you to keep your body in trim. Do this, and combined with the other elements we have mentioned, you will achieve physical congruence.

So there we are; we have covered Food and Exercise. It really is quite simple; yet like so many things in life it is not the complexity that stops us, just the awareness and FOCUS to take action. Exercise, like diet should not take willpower, because it should be a natural and desired part of your life.

Element 3) Sleep

The third element in being physically congruent is Sleep. Let me ask you: how well do you sleep at night? We all need different amounts. Are you getting enough sleep? If you are and you wake refreshed and energised then please feel free to skip this section. However, if your sleep is fitful or interrupted; if you have trouble switching off and getting to sleep without resort to pills or alcohol then stay with me. Lack of sleep is another symptom of your body telling you, you are **not congruent**.

It is a result of other elements where you are not congruent interfering with your energy patterns. Till we fix those elements, let us at least help you to get a decent night's sleep. You cannot be physically and therefore completely congruent if you are not getting enough sleep. As you know, lack of sleep leads to irritation, mistakes, tiredness, depression and a massive energy drain. It will greatly interfere with the use of the G.R.OW.T.H.S. U.P. model and your success in generating revenue and customers. Tired people cannot focus on their customers and have that natural conversation that is at the heart of the G.R.OW.T.H.S. U.P. P success.

It is a major block to being congruent, to letting our energy flow naturally; so let's see if we can help you get your good night's visit to slumberland.

One of the most common causes of being unable to drop off to sleep is the mind racing. If you can't switch off, you can't fall asleep. So let's try an exercise to help those of you that have that problem. What I suggest is that you review the exercise now, and then tonight, before you try to go to sleep, apply it to help yourself drop off. You will find it in the Appendix, "Exercises" under "Sleep".

Apart from the recommendation to exercise, let me offer some obvious points to help you sleep. Don't drink coffee or other stimulants less than four hours before you go to bed. Don't eat a full meal two to three hours before going to sleep; your body needs to be drug free and not digesting a heavy meal, otherwise all the energy and relaxation needed to help you sleep will be channelled elsewhere. Much as you might be tempted, do not work on your tablet or laptop just before you go to bed as recent research has shown this interferes with a good night's sleep. Do not succumb to having a TV in the bedroom as this causes over stimulation and sets up the psychological block to sleep by embedding the idea that the bedroom is not just for sleeping but also for entertainment. Making sure your curtains block the light effectively as a darkroom will help your body adjust to a sleep routine better. If you have trouble sleeping, why not try a warm bath before bed, meditation, or listening to a relaxation tape.

So there we are, we have looked at three of the elements; diet, exercise and sleep. There are two more essential elements in keeping your body physically congruent.

Elements 4/5) Freedom from Stress and Relaxation

The fourth and fifth elements are linked and they are: **being free from stress and knowing how to relax.** You may not know, but there is a physical cost to being stressed, especially if you are one of the many people who suffer from various forms of stress over a long period. We will look at the emotional and psychological cost later. For the moment consider this: every time you allow yourself to get stressed there are chemical and physical changes in your body. All these changes help in accelerating the aging process. So you need to realise that if you are one of those people who does suffer from stress, you are helping yourself to age faster and subjecting your body to an unhealthy state.

The whole subject of stress is a book and CD in itself and of course G.R.OW.T.H.S. U.P. will help take the stress out of one part of your life, which is generating revenue and customers. However, if stress exists in other parts of your life and interferes with your Congruence then read on. Suffice it to say, when you are stressed adrenaline and cortisol flood your body. These hormones are designed to prepare the body for what is known as the fight or flight response. That is, they speed up the body's metabolism, the heart beats faster, blood pressure increases (which is why some of you suffer from headaches when you get stressed) and the body goes into overdrive. That is all very well in small bursts, but over time it wears the body down. These chemicals also, by the way, suppress the immune system; so stressed people leave themselves open to a greater risk of illness.

At the same time, if you think back to when you have been stressed or uptight; maybe in your car, stuck in a traffic jam or on a crowded delayed train, you know what pushes your buttons. But here's the thing, remember how your body reacted. Were your hands clenched, shoulders taught, neck muscles tight, your stomach in knots? All of these are common physical manifestations of stress; and as I am sure you can realise, keeping those muscles under tension is bad for the body, burns energy unnecessarily and can lead to headaches and muscle pain.

As we have mentioned, even if you don't suffer from stress, being aware of the physical signs can be most useful in identifying if your customer is suffering from stress and allowing you to tailor your natural conversation to take that into account.

So, bottom line, stress has a physical toll. To be physically congruent you **need** to reduce or eliminate becoming stressed; you **need** to be able to relax. You cannot operate the G.R.OW.T.H.S. U.P. model in a stressed state as it will make it almost impossible to have the relaxed, positive, focused conversation that is at the heart of the model. So you can see how our fourth and fifth elements link. I believe that although we cannot control outside pressures of life, in most cases each of us has the capability to prevent that pressure turning into stress!

So I am going to give you a few tips and an exercise to help you avoid stress, stay relaxed and allow yourself to stay physically congruent. The added plus is that you will reduce your ageing process, and allow your body's energy to flow productively. Stress is one of the blocks you need to eliminate to be physically congruent.

Triggers

There are two parts to preventing pressure leading to stress. The first is to identify what causes you stress; because once identified you can either avoid the cause or trigger, or learn how to reduce its effect. The second part is learning how to relax if you do feel stress creeping up on you.

So let's explore the first part. What are your triggers? They are those things in life that cause you to get stressed. They might be physical (at work or at home), emotional or behavioural. For example, I find that overheated rooms start to get me very anxious. Once I realised that, I was able either to avoid such places or realise the source of the stress and leave the room before it became a problem. What about you? Is it confined spaces or crowds, noise or bright lights, computers that crash, your kids not tidying up their room or spending too long on the phone? What I suggest you do, now or when you are ready is, get a sheet of paper or a spreadsheet on your computer and write down all the physical, emotional or behavioural causes of your personal stress. Take your time; really think back to each cause – what actually triggered your stress? Write it down along with how it made you feel physically. Did you feel tense, muscles hunched, headache, whatever it may be? Once you have completed that exercise we will work on an exercise to help you deal with stress when you can't avoid the trigger. The exercise can be found in the Appendix, "Exercises".

Of course the stress of selling has already been eliminated from your life by applying G.R.OW.T.H.S. U.P. , so you are much closer to a relaxed state as one of the major possible triggers in your life has been removed: the frustration of not being able to stay relaxed and increase revenue and customers.

Well, whether the list has one thing in it or one hundred, if you can't avoid or reduce the cause, you need to know how to stop that pressure becoming stress and that is what these exercises are all about: relaxing whatever the situation, whatever the problem. One exercise which you can do walking, standing, sitting or lying is shown at the end of this book in the Appendix on Exercises where you will find a number of other tips you can also use to help you relax.

Practice relaxation as often as you need to and I assure you life's pressures will not get you stressed; and if your diet is right, you get enough exercise and sleep and you are free from stress and can relax, you will gain physical congruence, your body will be fully congruent and your energy flow will be uninterrupted. You will feel energised, happier and more positive about yourself and life in general and that's just physical congruence!

Physical congruence without psychological congruence is, however, not enough. It is by combining the two that the real benefits are achieved. So let's now turn to the second leg that congruence stands on, the psychological one.

Psychological congruence

When we are not congruent in our mind and soul what tends to happen is we fight against ourselves; and as we have seen before, that is a battle none of us can win. Think about when you were last out shopping. You saw something in a shop you really fancied, but you knew, in your mind, you didn't need it or could not really afford it. That battle between your logical mind and your illogical feelings or emotion happens when we are not congruent. By the way, who won?? The trouble is, whoever won, you lost. What do I mean? Well, if you resisted buying the item your logical mind felt good but your soul felt cheated. If you did buy the item then your soul and emotions felt temporarily fulfilled until your mind reminds you how weak you were not to resist. You see, when you fight yourself you never win! However, to continue the example, if you knew you needed an item for yourself, or as a gift for another; say you decided to donate to your favourite charity. Who would win then? Well, you knew how much you could afford and you donated that amount. Now, because mind and soul are congruent, you feel good about what you did. Not just for a brief moment, but forever. There is no downside because you were congruent; psychologically and emotionally in harmony. Your energy all flowed in one direction as opposed to pushing against itself.

For your mind and soul to be congruent there must be harmony between what you think and what you feel. If you are honest with yourself, and as we have seen before, you do need to be honest with yourself; you know when your mind and soul are in conflict. So, how do we gain congruence over mind and soul? How do we harmonise our psychological attitudes and emotional responses? It's all about practice and awareness. Be psychologically congruent and your goal of G.R.OW.T.H.S. U.P. will be easier, run smoother and energise you more.

To start the process, from now on, every time you go to do something and there is a conflict between what you intend and what you desire; or if you think a thought, and your "Conscience" or your soul tells you it's not right – **STOP! Take a deep breath and just take a few seconds to consider what it is causing the conflict.**

An example: you are in the office or at work and you are talking with your colleagues. As is normal, everyone is gossiping about someone else. You know a secret about the person under discussion. Your mind wants you to tell the group the secret but the voice of your soul, your conscience, reminds you that it is not really right to spread the information you learnt in confidence. Before you say anything, **STOP**. Take a breath and consider what is right for you, what will stop the conflict and bring congruence. It only takes a second and you know what is right. What is right is what is congruent.

Act on that and you will feel an internal rush of energy and satisfaction that far outweighs the temporary few seconds buzz of being popular in a conversation.

When you have done this once and taken this first step of stopping and considering before action, you will be on the path to being more in tune and more in touch with yourself, the real you. Every time you do this it will get easier and easier to connect with the real honest, hidden you that is your core you; your energised, honest, happy, congruent self. Each time you recognise the tug between the psychological you and the emotional you and stop and resolve the conflict and resume the congruence of mind and soul you will release real energy into your being. You will feel more satisfied and you will **know**: yes I am better than that (that being the conflict or quick fix).

As we quoted before: 'Awareness as always brings the present to life and that knowledge creates positive results."

If you practice this awareness, the STOP, Breath, and act honestly according to the congruent you (that is your conscience where mind and soul are in harmony); you will release that positive energy, feel better and be a better person. That will inevitably lead to a happier and healthier you. Believe me; people will begin to notice the difference. They will respect you more, listen to you more often, and whether you know it or not, react to the increased energy flow that such congruence brings.

Utilising G.R.OW.T.H.S. U.P. which is already your Focus, you will find no conflict in this area of your life as your congruence will flow naturally in a harmonious, relaxed, natural way as there is no conflict in what you are doing. The G.R.OW.T.H.S. U.P. model works best with and nurtures congruence by supporting and stimulating a relaxed, natural state to work in that allows uninterrupted energy flow and feelings of positive, happy dialogue.

So there we have it. Being congruent in body, mind and soul lets the energy flow freely through your physical, emotional and psychological self. Coupled to your Focus, Being Congruent will bring you a freedom to act, think and feel as well as give you a boost of energy every day you practice it. The wonderful thing is, the more you practice it the better and easier it gets. You will be healthier, happier and able to deal with life in a more positive and energised way and all around you will notice the difference. Your

G.R.OW.T.H.S. U.P. model will work in harmony with you and you with it, creating a natural, energised, positive, self-supporting environment to grow yourself and your business.

All we need to do now is add one more element and the formula is complete. That element is Control.

Control

Control is the script that allows the formula to work; it is the framework around which Focus and Congruence can function, the glue that holds it all together. So let me start this section with a story and a question. Question first. Do you ever feel that events are controlling you; that you feel powerless in the face of a string of disasters or mishaps? That you want to shout 'WHY ME?' I think there are times when it has happened to all of us, so I want to show you how often **you can** exert control if you want to.

To paraphrase the poet *God give me the strength to change what I can and accept that which I canno*t. For **Acceptance**, you may be surprised to learn, can also be a form of control, more of which later. Now to the story, which concerns a friend of mine, Stuart.

Stuart was always in a rush in the morning. The alarm would go off and, not being a morning person, he would press the snooze button to give himself another ten minutes of shut-eye. Then when the alarm rang again he would get up, shower, shave, dress, have a quick coffee and cereal, dash out the house and drive to work, cursing the traffic jam all the way. He usually arrived at work just on time or a few minutes late, would rush to open his PC and then spend an hour processing his emails, which made him late for the project he was looking after. This was very much the pattern of Stuart's life till one disastrous day.

Same scene; the alarm rang, he snoozed and got up, but as he did get up he stubbed his toe. The pain made his hand shake and, rushing to shave, he cut himself and then wasted more time covering it up. By the time he went downstairs for his coffee he was late. Rushing, not concentrating, he misjudged when he poured his coffee and spilt some on the work surface and floor. Cursing, he cleared it up and by the time he got to his car, now fifteen minutes late, he tried to start it but over revved it and it stalled. Finally, when he was on his way, traffic was crawling. He was angry, frustrated, and by the time he got to work late, was in a foul mood. Rushing to turn on his PC, he didn't wait for it to start up properly, pushed too many keys, and the PC crashed. At this point he said 'WHY ME?' and felt as if life had dealt him a crazy day. Of course, the rest of the day followed the same negative pattern.

So let me ask you, does any of that sound familiar? Are you saying we all get lousy days; what can you do? Well, it has happened to all of us but bear with me. Let's rerun the story, only this time inserting **Control** into it. You might be surprised at the outcome.

Let's start with the alarm going off and Stuart pressing the snooze button. He thinks he is getting an extra ten minutes of sleep. Actually he is **wasting** ten minutes and not really sleeping. So, control change number one. By the way, if this is you, maybe try this. When the alarm goes off, lie there and take a deep breath. That way you exert control from the start and are not just reacting to the alarm. Then get up. You have now bought yourself ten extra precious minutes instead of wasting them. OK, back to the story. So Stuart gets up and stubs his toe. If he was in control he would have known that the pain caused a shot of adrenaline and cortisol to course through his body, which speeded up his system (by the way, the reason for that is that any pain triggers and ancient fight or flight part of the brain, which releases these two chemical into the system). By taking a second, realising the drugs in his system will make him shaky, he exerts control and calms himself before doing anything else. In this state of control and awareness he would not have cut himself shaving or spilt the coffee because of his adrenalin-induced shaky hands. Now he can leave home ten minutes early, not fifteen minutes late. Traffic is lighter as it's earlier and is therefore less frustrating. He arrives at work early and in control, opens his PC normally and has extra time to deal with his emails. Now Stuart feels ahead of the day and In Control, and so his day naturally keeps getting better

Though this is a story, these are all real examples. We have far more control over our circumstances than we realise, as I hope you can see. Take a moment to consider how the rules of control in this story might apply to your life. Is there somewhere you could use these examples of control and indeed take more control of your life?

Regarding the G.R.OW.T.H.S. U.P. model, it is easy to see that the model works so much more powerfully when you are in control. It allows you to apply the skills that create the natural conversation in a much more positive mindset. It gives you the strength and energy to exercise the focus and congruence that allows your conversation to flow, enabling you to treat your customer as an individual with all your positive energy focused on and surrounding them. This combination of FCO^2 and the model will ensure each encounter is a positive and fulfilling one, thus helping you increase revenue and gain those extra customers.

I said earlier that **Acceptance** can be a form of control. Let's take the traffic jam as an example. We have all experienced them, sat in them, been frustrated by them. Now despite leaving early or late, trying alternate routes, sometimes we will still be stuck in that jam. The uncontrolled reactive, non-congruent reaction is to get frustrated, angry and nervous. Here is a situation you can do nothing about so why fight it? The controlled response is to say 'All right I'm in a jam, I can't do anything about it, so how can I use my time effectively?' With that attitude you are now in control and you can use the time to do breathing and relaxation exercises, listen to a CD, or the radio, or review what you need to do that day. What you do is up to you. The point is, you have accepted the problem over which you have no control and turned it into an opportunity to do what you want.

It means the jam, far from being a frustrating, energy-sapping experience is transformed into a useful positive space for you to relax; and so when you finally arrive at your destination you will be in a positive, congruent mood, ready for the day ass opposed to being in an angry, frustrated, nervous state, sapped of energy and happiness. Does that make sense and could you apply this to that and other situations? Do you see how control and acceptance can transform situations from negative, draining ones to positive, energising ones? Try it and see. I know you will feel the difference.

For example, concerning the G.R.OW.T.H.S. U.P. environment, you have spent ages getting an appointment with a really important client. Come the day, they either don't turn up or are late. You can either get frustrated and angry, sapping energy and strength, or see the situation as extra time when you can do all the other tasks you hadn't had time for. It is what in NLP we call a reframe, and it transforms an energy-sapping anger into a positive situation.

Just think about these examples and apply them to anything in your day that is relevant. Could you take control there? Of course you can. Try it next time you have a similar problem and you will feel the change. Like Congruence and Focus, the more you identify times to use it and practice it, the easier it becomes.

Physical and Psychological control

I hope you are getting the idea of how control will change your life and make it better. Let's just explore now a couple of different types of control: Physical control and Psychological control. Physical control is anything from working out in the gym for the full time you have allowed yourself, to not spitting out a tasteless piece of food in front of a guest. Physical control is about you controlling your body, not the other way around; even down to being ill on some occasions. How often do we feel "one degree under" yet convince ourselves we feel worse than we really do. Physical control allows us to realise how we really feel and to function effectively within real constraints; not bow to a sickness that is not as severe as we pretend.

That is of course linked to psychological control. If we control our mind then we will not succumb to the weak feeling of 'Oh, I'll stay in bed' when you know you should not, or not perform a task you know you should. Psychological control is about being honest and knowing that we can do more than we think we need to or are capable of doing.

The ultimate examples are: a mother lifting a heavy weight to free her child when normally she could never lift it; or going without sleep for long periods, say when nursing a sick child, or being in the emergency services or the military. I am sure you can think of many other examples yourself, can't you? The point is we can either allow circumstances to dictate our actions and give in to self-defeating assumptions such as 'I can't swim, write, or pass that exam', **or we can take control, and with focus and congruence honestly decide to take positive, honest action.**

So, there we have it "**Control**". The framework for the formula, the map that shows the direction we have to go, the frame within which we will succeed. Control is about taking positive, active control of your life whatever the circumstance. It's about taking responsibility and removing blame. You are in control, if you want to be; no one and nothing else can prevent or block that.

So as you can see, applying G.R.OW.T.H.S. U.P. is made so much easier if you also apply the FCO^2 Formula. Once you have Focus, Congruence and Control you will have so much more energy and time to make G.R.OW.T.H.S. U.P. work and will feel relaxed and stress-free at the same time. This will help you effortlessly generate revenue and more customers and give you the peace of mind to grow and develop the other areas of your business.

Now it is time to take the formula and the model and apply them directly to ensure your G.R.O.W.T.H.S. U.P.

Section 3 Applying G.R.O.W.T.H.S. U.P.

12 INTRODUCTION AND STATION 1 "DISCOVER"

As you will see, to apply our model effectively and practically you will need to join me on a journey of DisCRETioN. That journey will take the theory and thrust it into the real world, where you operate, to ensure your G.R.OW.T.H.S. U.P. really happens.

Our journey of DisCRETioN. includes the ability to:

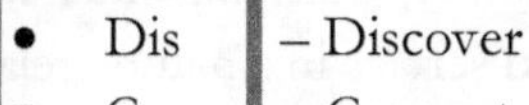

- Dis – Discover
- C – Connect
- R – (Build) Rapport
- E – Exchange
- T..io – Tie up a Transaction
- N – Nurture

We will look at each stage individually, but first…

Up till now we have looked at defining the theoretical framework of the G.R.OW.T.H.S U.P. model to create that natural conversation and remove hassle, fear and stress. We have supplemented that with tools to help you understand the environment within which to operate the model and how best to utilise it using the skills and formula you now have and can practice, till they become, as we stated, unconscious competence.

The tools, to recap, to help you with the model were to, S.M.I.L.E., where we looked at starting with a smile, making eye contact, individualising the exchange, making sure that you looked closely, listened intently and lead gently, and then engaged with your customer. In this chapter, we will apply these techniques into the practical environment you may we working in to help you gain and keep more customers and increase revenue.

We will do this by taking you and your customer on a journey to success using the G.R.O.W.T.H.S U.P. model at each stage and incorporating the relevant skills and tools like S.M.I.L.E.

In this journey of DisCRETioN we will also revisit and utilise our N.I.C.E. C.H.A.T.

By focusing on being natural and individual while making sure we clarify the exchange; by being in alignment with our customer, clarifying their need, highlighting the value to them of our product and service in a natural relaxed way, we will agree to our exchange and ideally tie up a transaction leading to revenue growth.

We will ensure that we are aware of the N.O.I.S.E. that distorts our conversation and apply practical examples to counter it, so we can have a clear, unambiguous, focused, natural chat. We will create an environment to counter the negative expectations and obstinate beliefs, while focusing on our own and their image.

In addition, by staying on the right PA.T.H. we can, by painting a picture, telling a story and having that natural conversation, generate the revenue and customers we need, without hassle while uplifting our performance. This is while being happy and applying the FCO^2 Formula to stay focused, congruent and in control.

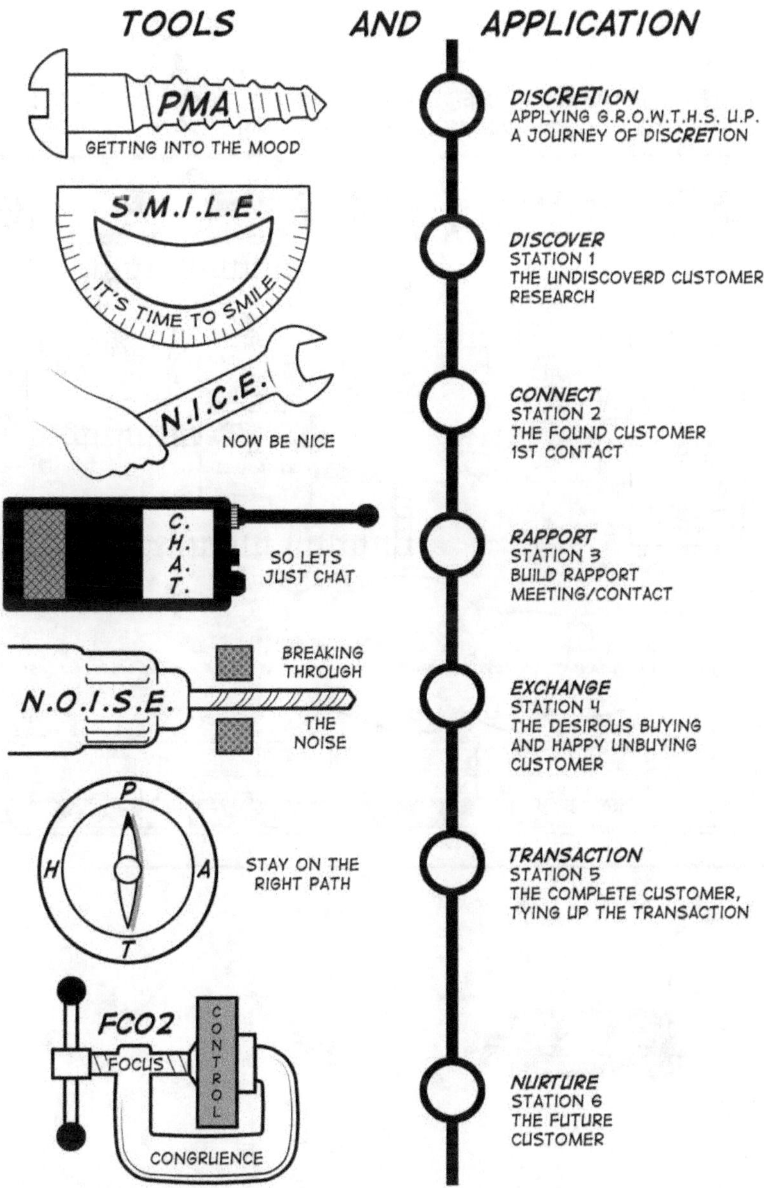

That is our journey of DisCRETioN that we embark on now. Enjoy the ride.

To help you with this journey the diagram gives you an indication of where we will be going.

YOURS AND THE CUSTOMER JOURNEY USING THE G.R.OW.T.H.S. U.P. MODEL. ALL YOU NEED IS DIS.C.R.E.TIO.N.

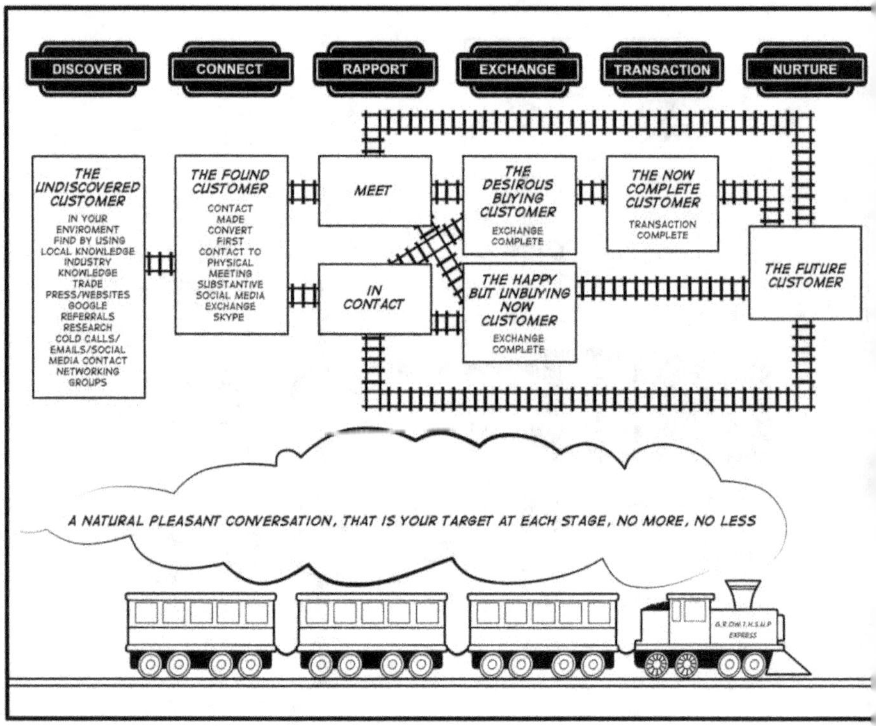

So let us first look at what I call the "undiscovered customer" and the first station on our journey to success, the one named "Discover". The G.R.O.W.T.H.S. U.P. model is about generating revenue and customers without hassle. Of course part of that is how you deal with existing customers, or the ones that just walk into your place of business or contact you direct. We will apply the model to those, in our stations from Connect, through Rapport, Exchange to Transaction and Nurture.

However, I thought it important to show you how you can even apply the model to help you find new resources and customers without feeling the pressure that often is associated in old sales styles by "cold calling", or aggressive marketing to "Prospects" to turn them into "Closes".

For any business from plumber to programmer, carpenter to chartered accountant, technology has created a wealth of resources to find customers, market the business and maintain contact with people interested in your product or service. It has also, as it has evolved and keeps on evolving, created almost too many channels and too much information, so it is hard to filter out some of it to be able to focus on what is really important.

The technique at this station of "Discover" is to use our model to make the acquisition of customers and resources as relaxed and hassle-free as possible while utilising the technology to our advantage. Bearing in mind that our approach, the model's focus, is on the individual, it is about respect, care and helping; not quick fixes, rapid closes or exploitation.

Whatever your business, whether it is retail in a small or medium-sized shop or providing a service from an office or home, or anything in between such at click and pick, you have two major choices at this "Discover" station when it comes to finding extra resources and customers. You can either be passive or proactive. Being passive means you run your business in hope. You might be lucky, and, if you are well-established, waiting for business to come to you may be sufficient. Yet I suspect you wouldn't mind boosting your footfall or through flow of customers. Of course, referrals are the best way to get new business and we will look at them in more detail when new get to our "Nurture" station. If you are a shop in the high street or business in a shopping centre, casual customers just walking in is important, but relying on just that resource could leave you short of the revenue you need, especially when it is possible to boost your pool of resources without hassle or stress.

That is what I want to discuss at this station and how the model applies.

Using the internet and other resources divides itself also into passive and proactive elements.

Advertising

Let's get rid of the passive first as it does not need our model to operate except in the design and placement. Passive is advertising. You put your advert out there and hope for a response. In the current environment the good news is that you can put your advert out in a lot of places for free or minimal cost. The trouble is, it means you are waiting for someone to see it and act upon it. For completeness, and depending on your business, look at this list of possible locations that you might want to consider placing your ad. It is of course not complete as new players emerge all the time.

I should also mention here two ways to put your information out there and which straddle the line between passive and proactive: using Public Relations (PR) and "thought leadership" pieces or articles. Using a PR company is expensive. However, if you have a specific project or concept that is time sensitive and needs plenty of national or international press coverage this is one of the best ways to achieve it.

Thought leadership is the name for putting out a piece, whether on social media or other internet or regular channels, that does not advertise your product or service but provides the public with insights into the environment that your product or service sits in: for example, a health company providing an ad on TV or on Facebook about the benefits of going to a gym or losing weight. The piece is informative and educational and is designed to stimulate. The only mention of the company is at the end where who wrote or sponsored the piece is listed. This is a good way to build awareness and can, over time, build interest and loyalty.

List of possible advertising locations:

- **Global**
- **Twitter**
- **Facebook**
- **LinkedIn**
- **Instagram**
- **Google**

- **YouTube**
- **Your own website**

- **National**
- **Yell**
- **Thompson**
- **National papers**
- **Trade websites**
- **Networking groups 4Networking, BNI, etc.**
- **Trade shows and exhibitions**

- **Local**
- **Yell**
- **Thompson**
- **Local websites**
- **Local networking groups**
- **Local papers' websites and hard copy**
- **Trade shows and exhibitions**
- **Shop windows**
- **Council offices**
- **Flyers**
- **Markets**

This is not the place to go through each of these options in detail, as there are plenty of resources available on the web to help you. If you do have a specific question to ask me, that you cannot find an answer to, please feel free to email me at growthsup@gmail.com and I will endeavour to help you.

That said, there are certain areas where our model and tools apply. We are looking to stimulate interest in us in a non-aggressive, positive manner, building connections for the future. So according to our model, the ads you place should reflect that softer focus. You are stimulating interest, not grabbing an audience.

So the G.R.OW.T.H.S. U.P. model suggests placing ads where they can do long-term good; Facebook, websites, trade pages, for instance, where at low or minimal cost you can build a reputation, a brand and an interest in a way that attracts customers positively, so that when they do connect, your natural conversation and N.I.C.E. C.H.A.T. will seem to be a seamless extension of the ads and communications you have already planted in the wider environment.

From the start there should be congruence in all your communications, from advertising and thought leadership pieces, through to more proactive measures, which we will look at next. You want to create a smooth-flowing stream of consciousness, not a swirling, raging river running through the hazards of rapids and gorges.

Research

So having briefly touched on the passive let us now spend some time applying the model to the proactive acquisition of resources and customers. This comes under the generic heading "Research" in our "Discover" station, which is about looking for the UNDISCOVERED customer. Many of the locations we mentioned in our list above can also be used for proactive research to find both the undiscovered customer and to make first contact and so taking us to the second station on our journey – "Connect".

Let us divide the research into local, national and global, physical and digital, and see how the model can help us in each environment.

Local Physical

- **Local friends and colleagues –**
  There is a concept that has been around a long time that I call the 3 circles of connection.

The first circle is your closest family and friends; the second, business acquaintances and casual connections; and the third, the rest of the public in general. When researching to find that "undiscovered customer" it is always best to begin with the inner circle and work out. I am sure many of you have already come across this approach.

However, it is amazing how many people, because of the fear engendered by old selling techniques, are afraid to approach what could be their most valuable resource. The good news is that using the G.R.OW.T.H.S. U.P. model you can practice having that "natural conversation" on a sympathetic audience and reconnect with your closest connections in a positive and non-threatening way. You might be amazed by the results.

To practice your G.R.OW.T.H.S. U.P. model, become relaxed and familiar with it and to gain the greatest initial impact for your business, the first circle of your family and friends, where relevant, will provide you with an initial source of customers and revenue. This environment is the least difficult and most supportive in enabling you to hone your skills and see the results.

The second circle consists of your existing business contacts and more casual acquaintances. Again, because you already have a connection here, re-establishing communication using the model, in a relaxed, positive way, should yield results more quickly and with less effort.

If you are looking for an excuse to renew contact then why not be honest and say that you are using a new model to help grow your business and you would be grateful for their help and support while you develop it. Most people like to be consulted and needed and this combined with the model's N.I.C.E. C.H.A.T. and relaxed atmosphere can greatly boost actual customers among existing contacts.

The third circle is basically everyone else you can find and come into contact with. For example:

People who call in.

If you have a physical location, a shop or office, for example, you will always have people just walking in. Obviously it will be different if you have a coffee shop or a legal practice, a pub or a furniture shop. However, the model and the principle remains the same. All you are doing, whoever walks in, is aiming to have a natural conversation; that S.M.I.L.E. and N.I.C.E. C.H.A.T, treating them as individuals, with respect and interest and building that rapport. We will look at this in a lot more detail when we come to our "Rapport" station.

The point is every person who walks through your door is not just a potential customer but also an ambassador for your brand. You never know who they are, what their connections might be or how important they are; so treat everyone the right way and even if they don't buy, as long as they receive respect and good service they will tell others. Apply the model and your business will maximise every opportunity and increase revenue accordingly.

Just one story to illustrate the point: a friend of mine runs a coffee shop, which I regularly visit. On day I was sitting there when a shabbily-dressed but very polite elderly man came in. The staff treated him with respect, were considerate, and made sure he was comfortable, even though he only wanted a small coffee. He stayed a while and left thanking them and they thought no more of it. The next week he came back with ten other people who were down for the wedding of one of his grandchildren. They bought lunch, drinks and spent a considerable amount of money. Not only that, but they put a message on Facebook about how much they liked the experience. You see, you never know where your business comes from, so treat everyone the same, have that natural conversation, be focused, respectful and interested.

Your local high street

This is also in your third circle or maybe even your second. The point is, you probably have some knowledge of the people there and again it is easier just to pop in for a natural chat and, where relevant, drop off your card or just mention what you are doing and again, if relevant, whether you can help. It's just a natural conversation, no more. You never know what might come of it.

Local markets

If you have a local market, you might want to consider, if relevant to your business, booking a spot for a couple of occasions. It will give you relaxed exposure, allow you to chat to lots of people, and again all you need to is show off your product or service and have a relaxing chat. No pressure, no push and you could easily raise interest and gain new contacts. Usually the cost is low so the potential return could be fantastic – just by having a

N.I.C.E. C.H.A.T. and a S.M.I.L.E. The model works here too.

Local networking groups

Most locations have local networking groups such as BNI, 4Networking or other county-based groups or business circles. These are usually not too expensive to join, or at least to attend one or two meetings or to go along as a guest. These are a great way to meet that potential undiscovered customer in a relatively supportive environment and have a natural conversation. The point about these groups is that everyone is there to sell their product or service, so it is easier to have that conversation without being worried. It is important to note, however, that it is not for everyone. It is usually early, a breakfast meeting, and you are expected to stand up and give a short, 60 second or so, presentation. That said; it is a good source of local contacts.

Local radio

The growth in local internet stations may be a good source of getting your name out to the local community. If you can offer yourself as an expert in your field and do a short slot on your subject you will be also able to mention your company and this might bring in enquiries. Of course, you need to know your subject, not just talk about your product or service, and be prepared to talk on the radio.

Stalls in shopping centres

Most shopping centres allow, with permission, small pop-up stalls for a day. This is a good way to make contact with a larger number of third circle people, especially if the location is not directly where you have your shop or office, or is in a much better location for attracting interest. Again, this is an easy and cost-effective way to do research and find that "undiscovered customer".

Remember, according to our model you are just having a natural conversation, a S.M.I.L.E. and a N.I.C.E. C.H.A.T, so it is a nice, easy way to meet people; and if they show interest get their contact details for the future. Remember to have a stand and poster along with some marketing material. This is your brand displayed so remember that 'as you only get one chance to make a first impression', make sure it looks crisp and professional.

Creating local events

It may be that you don't have access to the above, or decide you want a more focused approach. Hiring a local hall or venue and presenting your product or service for an hour or two can be an effective method to obtain contacts and potential customers. Be aware that depending on how large your local community is, you may need to invest in advertising to attract interest, such as in local papers or posters in shops. Of course you will also have to be comfortable speaking to a large group of strangers. Nevertheless, this is a useful way to get your name out there and find more of the "undiscovered customer". You won't have to sell anything, just have that natural conversation with a larger group. This is not the place to go into the subject of how to present to larger groups. However, if any of you do have any concerns or questions, please feel free to contact me at: growthsup@gmail.com.

Local digital

That was a review of some of the local, physical options open to you at your first station "Discover" to find your "undiscovered customer". Now it is time to turn to a few local digital options that can also help in your proactive research.

Local websites/emails

Just as there are local networking groups and local markets, most business communities, especially among small- and medium-size businesses, have local versions of national websites, or specific local, county or town web addresses.

Many of these can be found on social media sites such as Facebook or Twitter. It is often free or very cheap to post a message on their sites explaining your product or service and listing your contact details. The other advantage to joining one of these sites or groups is that you also have access to their members. Just as in the networking groups, this enables you to send out specific messages or emails to them, as well as posting on the website.

Remember our model and being congruent. Do not sell aggressively, have a digital version of a N.I.C.E. C.H.A.T. Explain how you can help, what you offer and invite a response. If you can include a picture or video, so much the better. Keep it simple and brief and to the point.

In any emails you send, again, as they are unsolicited, be relaxed and gentle in your language. Treat the recipient as an individual, using their name and offer help.

Local newspapers

Both daily and weekly newspapers are an excellent source of contact information for finding your "undiscovered customers". Local news will highlight individuals who have changed circumstances or received new contracts or awards. New businesses will often be listed in detail, with a paragraph on them highlighting their product or service and the names of the owners or managers.

You have the option, where relevant, to call round or send a letter or email congratulating them and just introducing yourself – no more. You or they can then decide to follow up. That will move you to your second station, "Connect" and converting the research into a first contact and a "found customer".

So there we have one of the best sources of increasing your customer base, proactive research in your local community. As you can see, the G.R.OW.T.H.S. U.P. model applies here, allowing you, without stress or pressure, to have that relaxed physical or digital conversation; giving you the opportunity to practice your G.R.OW.T.H.S. U.P. model and your S.M.I.L.E. and N.I.C.E. C.H.A.T without any hassle or pressure – and possibly gaining new sources of revenue and more potential customers.

Now we are going to briefly review some national and global research resources you might want to utilise; again using the model of a natural conversation and a congruent, positive approach.

National/Global Physical

Exhibitions, events, shows

If you decide you want a national or global presence and wish to pursue a physical, direct approach, then there are some avenues open to you. However, the more national and global you get in the physical environment, the costlier it becomes. Nevertheless, in the right location, the exposure and source of contacts from your third circle can help find that "undiscovered customer".

The obvious best physical location is a national or international exhibition or event where you can either have a stand or booth, or use the opportunity to visit and find out who your competition is and who your potential customers might be.

If you decide on a booth you will need to book it well ahead of time, up to a year in some cases, and of course ensure your material is of the highest quality. If you go to the event to see who is there, be aware that all the booth holders are interested in promoting their products so do not sell yours. Utilise the model and have that natural conversation. You will make good contacts, understand the environment better and have a positive encounter with stallholders and other visitors. Make sure you have plenty of business cards. Be aware that you will be contacted by anyone you gave your card to; that after all is the purpose of the event, and something you can take advantage of if you have a stall or booth.

Make sure your follow-up is made within a month of the show or event. Of course, you must realise, that many others will be doing the same, so make sure your contact is relaxed and friendly and you will get a better take-up than an aggressive sales call would.

Networking groups

Just as we discussed in the local environment, most networking groups share nationally; and once you are connected with the local group it is often easy to attend national events as well as other groups in other parts of the country. There are also networking events that are purely national; these are usually more expensive to attend, but are well worth it if relevant to your sector or business. The approach is the same; use the model, have that natural conversation and if necessary, be prepared for a 60-second or two-minute presentation on your subject, product or service. National events are a great place to network and pick up contacts and find that "undiscovered customer".

National/Global Digital

Here nearly all your local digital and advertising digital environments can be used for research and obtaining contacts, helping you find that "undiscovered customer".

Twitter

You can have a Twitter presence that is local, national or globally oriented. Putting out information in this format and following relevant people, businesses, organisations and groups can lead to them following you and providing you with potential customers. Remember, Twitter feeds are short and to the point and should be interesting and informative, or where relevant, humorous. Stay congruent; keep your message relevant and positive.

Facebook

Just as this is a good local source of information and message distribution, so it can be used in the national or global environment. Pitch your message wider; befriend those in the national and global arena and join Facebook pages with a wider reach. All of this will give you access to a vast pool of information on businesses and contacts that could become your "undiscovered customer". Keep the messages congruent, positive and interesting. Being slightly quirky or humorous might well help people liking and sharing your message.

LinkedIn

This is an excellent professional networking platform and ideal for placing your own or your company profile. By joining and contributing to groups and publishing posts, while connecting to relevant others in the community, you can greatly increase your contact base. You can see what others are talking about and what competitors and potential customers are saying and linking in to. This is a national and international tool for research and finding customers, associates and help. It is free to join and has a wide coverage and large number of contributors.

YouTube

It is easy and free to have your own YouTube site. Here, you can publish and upload your own videos on your subject, product or service. If you look at what is out there you will see a vast range of topics is covered. This is an interesting and free way to put your message out there and invite contacts. Use the model, keep it positive and relevant and treat your audience with interest and respect. Offer help rather than demand purchase.

Your own website

If you create your own website make sure you have a contact page so that people who visit it can contact you easily. If you wish to extend coverage to gain more contacts then, by making sure you take advantage of Google search engines using their various schemes, you can boost traffic to your site. Be aware, this of course costs money. You can also link your site to other websites that you may connect with, if they let you, as well as featuring it on Facebook, LinkedIn, Twitter, and so on. All of these will help you gain more national and global contacts depending on how you pitch your website. There are many companies out there that offer free or cheap help to host and design such a site, such as 1:1, which I use.

So there we have it – the first chapter in applying G.R.O.W.T.H.S. U.P. As you can see – in this our first station "Discover", on our journey to convert the "undiscovered customer" into a nurtured resource – there are a range of passive and proactive resources you can tap into to find the "undiscovered customer" and decide whether you want to make first contact and turn that potential resource into a "found customer" that you can meet and develop. That is the subject of the next chapters, as we arrive at the next two stations on our journey, which are "Connect" and "Rapport".

What is important to note is that our G.R.OW.T.H.S U.P. model, incorporating the tools and skills of a S.M.I.L.E. and a N.I.C.E. C.H.A.T. are applicable even at this first stage. They feature even more heavily as we make a connection, build rapport, conduct an exchange, complete a transaction and nurture our customer for the future. So let us continue on our journey of ensuring your G.R.OW.T.H.S. U.P.!

13 STATION 2 "CONNECT"

You have now, through your research and answers to your adverts, blogs and messages, identified the "undiscovered customer". Now it is time to transform them into the "found customer" at our second station, "Connect", where first contact is made, reinforced and developed into a meaningful connection; a strong first contact that leads to a meeting or powerful communication that is the next station on our journey building "Rapport".

Obviously the lines between all these stations on our journey are flexible and feed into one another with overlaps and repetitions. The DisCRETioN model is there to simplify the process, illustrate each step and how the G.R.O.W.T.H.S. U.P. model can be actually applied at each station and point on the journey.

To continue…

I see the first contact at this station of "Connect" as converting the awareness of the potential customer through some form of communication into a substantive meeting or connection.

Which type of research generated this potential "found customer" will determine how that first contact is made and developed. Let us look at several scenarios and apply the G.R.O.W.T.H.S. U.P. model to each.

<u>The first set of scenarios is First contact where the "found customer" comes to you.</u>

These should be the easiest to convert into a meaningful contact, meeting or connection moving us rapidly to our next station on the journey building "Rapport". Though each case is individual there are some general rules for the model that apply universally here.

For every "found customer" that you deal with, of course treat them with respect, as an individual, allowing you to build towards the rapport that will take you further down your journey. In first contact, that means listening to them, using their name, identifying yourself clearly, endorsing and acknowledging the connection that recommended them and beginning to build a safe environment for them to purchase whatever it is they are interested in.

First of all a Referral.

Though we will look at asking for and cultivating referrals in detail in our chapter "Nurture", the last station on our journey, here we deal with them contacting you. If they walk in, phone, email or contact you by social media, because someone you already have as a customer has referred them to you, the new-found customer has less noise to distract them. Your brand reputation and credibility has a ready-made foundation. This first contact should be handled with care and respect using our G.R.O.W.T.H.S. U.P. model. Whatever the method of communication they initiate, thank them for contacting you, acknowledge who has recommended them as a valued customer and begin a natural conversation to understand their needs and how you can help. If it is a digital connection, where appropriate transform it into a physical one by inviting them to your office, shop or place of business, only if they have the time and interest to do so. Otherwise let them chat with you about their needs. This "Connect" rapidly moves itself into the third station on our journey, building "Rapport" and setting up a physical meeting or another communication. In many cases that one meeting or call will result in a complete journey of exchange, transaction and nurture.

One of the reasons this can happen so rapidly is that the referred customer has the most positive feeling for listening and completing a transaction. They feel safe. That safety is a natural consequence of the G.R.O.W.T.H.S. U.P. model, of building rapport and treating your customer with respect, care, and as an individual; and understanding and breaking through their N.O.I.S.E., as we explored previously.

Next the Walk-in

Almost as good as a referral, depending on what your business is, is the walk-in. The mere fact that the potential "found customer" has decided to enter your establishment already allows you a considerable advantage. Their level of N.O.I.S.E. will be less as they have made a positive choice to walk in. Taking advantage of that by treating every single person who walks in as a potential "found customer" and not an intrusion to your business will allow you to use the model and S.M.I.L.E. and begin your N.I.C.E. C.H.A.T.

Even if the person entering your premises does not look or sound like your preconceived notion of a "found customer", treat each one of them as if they were. Be helpful and respectful, see them as an individual and enter into a natural conversation. Using the open questions we have learnt and being focused, begin the process of converting the "found customer" and your first contact into a substantial meeting, building the rapport that is the next station on our journey. In the case of the referral, walk-in or call-in, the process from "Connect" to "Rapport" is brief as your "found customer" has already shown an interest in your business and its service or product.

Then there is the Call-in

This is someone who has heard of you through some means and is interested in knowing more. Again, their NOISE level will be turned down as they already have some familiarity with you, or your product or service and are interested enough and trusting enough to call you. That is the good news. However because it is a call then you are missing some of the total package to allow you to have the real conversation. We look at this in more detail in "Rapport". Suffice it to say here that in any interaction between two people the message is conveyed and rapport built in three main ways: body language, voice – which includes tone, pitch and pace – and the actual words used. Take a minute to think about what you believe the percentages of these three would be in influencing that conversation, that connection.

You may be surprised at this model.

The point is that in the call the conversation has lost 55% of its content so you will have to work extra hard to have your natural conversation and ensure you convert that first contact into something more. Whether it all takes place in one call or you manage to invite that person in for a face-to-face meeting, or another call, or complete the exchange and transaction there and then; you will need to understand that the mechanics of your natural conversation need to be fine-tuned to the fact that you have lost 55% of your interaction, and will need the other two to work harder to make up for it.

In any event, this call is more likely to lead to the next station "Rapport" as the person has called you. Whatever the outcome, your target is the natural conversation and leaving the person on the other end feeling good, positive and an individual whether or not you proceed to the next station. We will look at using the phone to build rapport more in our next chapter.

On of the many ways you will receive interest is by email.

The advantage of an email is its immediacy and ease of use. The problem with it is its expectation and lack of emotional content. If someone has emailed you they are showing an interest. However you don't know the real level of emotional interest; it could be far less than a call-in or a drop-in or it could be the same. Email does not allow you to really gauge the emotional level behind the message.

Indeed, one must be careful as there is only 7% of the message to work with. In other words we only have the words, and no voice or body language. So it is important that we do not impress our own needs and emotions on to such a limited communication. If we are not in a positive state, it is really easy to view a neutral email as negative. The other point about emails is that unlike calls or drop-ins, there are expectations as to how long it take to answer. In our more connected world, people expect answers much quicker than they used to. When letters were the main form of communication for business, it could take three to five days to deliver and the same to reply and receive the response.

Now if you don't receive an answer to your email within a few hours, or a day at the most, you feel irritated. So, make sure you set up a system to answer emails within a specific time period; whatever you deem to be appropriate. Respond personally with the person's name and use the level of formality they do. Where possible, try to amplify their need if it is not clear by asking open questions and having a more stilted but natural conversation and using the model, in a relaxed way, to see if you can suggest a call or meeting; or suggest that dropping into your premises is the best way of helping them and satisfying their need. Obviously, if this is geographically impossible, go for a call. Even better, and we will look at this next, see if you can go for a Skype call because as that utilises voice and visual communication that converts 7% ie words only, into nearly 100% of a communication.

In any event, make sure the mail is positive, respectful, clear and relaxed and aim to convert it to a meaningful first contact by setting up (in order of best practice) a face-to-face meeting, a Skype, call or another email to help them with their query.

If you have a website where they can order the product direct, you could point them there. The problem with that is you might fulfil that order but not build a personal relationship for the future. Obviously it depends on the product or service, the speed of need, the geography and logistics.

That leads us nicely to the area of social media enquiries via Facebook, LinkedIn, YouTube, Twitter and Skype[both telephone by internet and now text and messaging social media] and how you can respond to these.

Social media has become and is becoming the communications method of choice for more and more people, especially but not exclusively if your audience is younger. Social media has an intimacy, immediacy and personalisation not found in emails. If you have a presence on social media with a Facebook page or a Twitter account – if professional, a LinkedIn profile – and maybe a YouTube channel to put out videos of your service, product or thought leadership piece, then you may receive enquiries that way. If you have a Skype account you can receive enquiries via that route too. As we shall see, it is an excellent system for making return contact.

So if you receive a message via social media, reply to it in a personal, friendly and focused way using the natural conversation and our G.R.O.W.T.H.S. U.P. model. By replying in a timely manner and keeping the connection focused, personal, relaxed and positive, you will be able to find out what the need is quickly and easily and convert the first contact into the next level of "Rapport" easily and smoothly. This may be, by continuing the conversation on the social media platform, or suggesting a follow up; as in the email, by a visit, call or indeed a Skype call. The advantage of a Skype call is, it's free, [except to landlines and mobiles] most people now have access to it and it allows you to see and hear your customer. This means you can more rapidly have a complete natural conversation and build "Rapport" by making that meaningful first contact into something more.

Converting a Facebook enquiry or Twitter response into something more works well as the query has come from someone already relaxed with the social media platform. If it is a professional LinkedIn message, you may need more time to convert it to a personal email, Skype call or face-to-face meeting, but the principle is the same.

Use the model and have a natural, relaxed, positive conversation at the level of formality or friendliness of your customer. Convert their interest into a strong first contact with a follow-up of some kind, according to the rules mentioned before. At the least, and if nothing more, respond in a timely manner and leave the person feeling that you were interested, respectful, saw them as an individual and wanted to help. This will leave them feeling positive even if the contact progresses no further. They are more likely to contact you again and tell others about your attitude and approach.

There are vast resources on the web on how to maximise social media, so if this is something you need more help with please look there, or if you have a specific question about the model and this area, contact me on: growthsup@gmail.com or via my website www.growthsup.co.uk.

Which leads us nicely to a follow-up enquiry from your website.

Here, the person contacting you has found your website, seen more detail of what you do or produce and is still interested in knowing more. Follow this up quickly, usually with an email, unless they have provided a phone number or social media location. Answer any specific queries and at the same time begin a natural, relaxed, conversation to see, if appropriate, whether you can build to the next level of "Rapport" by suggesting that a follow-up call, Skype call or personal visit would allow you to serve them even better.

Whatever you decide, make the first contact positive, practical, personal. Treat each enquiry as unique and construct the reply so as to give the person a feeling of warm energy. Show that you see them as individuals and are happy to help in any way you can. Make sure you also offer them alternative ways to contact you, with your telephone number or location, if relevant.

Finally, you might receive a response from a radio slot or newspaper ad.

The same rules apply here as they do to the website follow-up. They are seeking you out proactively after hearing or seeing more about you. Use the communication method they provide to begin the natural conversation. Your target is that natural conversation and converting first contact into the next level of building rapport. Suggest a follow-up of some kind, while answering their query in a polite, respectful manner. Treat the enquiry as unique and the person as an individual. If a newspaper ad from a local paper, or response from local radio, suggest a drop-in to your premises or visit, where appropriate. If a national newspaper or radio, then use the website rules of follow-up and aim for a meeting if appropriate – and if not, a call or Skype connection.

So there we have the easier part of our second station "Connection": converting an enquiry into a strong first contact that will either move you down the line to our next station "Rapport", or leave the enquirer with a strong, positive feeling about you and your product or service, setting up a future possible connection.

Now we have to examine the harder side of "Connection" where your research has identified the "undiscovered customer" and it is you that has to proactively seek them out, make the first connection and where possible, move them down the line to our next station "Rapport", still using our model to help you in that task.

<u>Your research identifies the "found customer".</u>

Some general rules apply here too, both in using the model and in how and when you make contact. So, how to contact, when to contact, what to say, how to develop that contact using our model are considered next.

General rules

First, be aware of any N.O.I.S.E. that might exist. Make sure you are aware of the wider environment as well as any other information you might have on the potential "found customer" before you initiate first contact. There is a saying: 'Time spent in reconnaissance is never wasted.' In other words, before you initiate first contact with your "undiscovered customer" find out everything you can about them. 'You only get one chance to make a first impression', so make sure that impression is the best it can be; and that you use the G.R.O.W.T.H.S. U.P. model to its maximum, applying where possible the skills of S.M.I.LE., N.I.C.E. C.H.A.T., P.A.T.H. and Breaking through the N.O.I.S.E.

This combination of detailed research and applying the model will give you the best chance to convert the "undiscovered customer" to a "found customer", and move the connection on to building "Rapport". There is a great difference between sending an impersonal blanket email to a hundred possible contacts from a trade show and linking to them individually on LinkedIn, Facebook or Twitter. Even a personal email, targeted directly, will have a massive difference in impact compared to a generalised mailshot. It is more time-consuming but it is time well spent. Results will prove quality is better than quantity, even though it is important to spread your message widely, but intelligently.

In doing your research prior to first contact, these are some of the factors of your contact you should review: name, role, company, product, service, location and contact details are the basic ones. On top of that, when you are about to contact them have you considered what is the best time? And what is the best method? Before you make contact, is there anything that might be affecting their business that would mean your first contact might be missed or ignored because of other pressing situations? For example, a train strike might prohibit a business from opening or functioning properly; an economic slowdown or difficult international situation might prevent the business from focusing on you. Imagine trying to have a conversation with a tour company focused on Greece during the June to August 2015 period; or a logistics company transitioning through Calais in the summer of 2015.

In addition, you might notice it is your contact's birthday; or there is some other event or anniversary of the person, the company or family you might wish to acknowledge. If you were approaching someone you found in a newspaper ad who was celebrating 25 years in the same business or location, acknowledging that would be important, as would a Facebook message saying they had just launched a new product or taken on a new member of staff. The more knowledge you have the more you can make your natural conversation relevant and make that first contact personal, unique and individual, thus distinguishing yourself from all the other noise they might receive.

Regarding the general timing of social media chat replies, emails and telephone calls (as opposed to social media posts which can be posted at any time to be reviewed at leisure), there are times in the day and during the week that emails, telephone contact or instant messenger may not be appropriate whereas posting a note on social media may be suitable.

For example, in the Western world, Monday morning and Friday afternoons are not great for telephone calls or emails. People are usually busy at work at the one and winding down at the other. According to research Tuesday at 11:00 is best for emails: the Monday apathy has gone and by Tuesday people are more likely to look at and answer emails quickly. Telephone calls to business personnel between 08:00 and 12:00 and 14:00 and 16:30 Tuesday to Thursday often tend get a better response. This is unless you know a senior manager or potential customer is in early or late and it is easier to get straight through to them as no receptionist or secretary might field your call.

Please note that if you are dealing with the Middle East, Sunday is a regular working day and Friday and Saturday are days when no business is usually conducted. If you are in contact with the west coast of the USA or Asia, or Australia from Western Europe, be aware of the considerable time differences.

Facebook and other social media posts can be posted at any time, as people will access it when they want. However, specific messages should be replied to within a short space of time after being received and certainly no more than a day later.

Twitter is more immediate, so I would suggest Monday before 08:00, or perhaps if you have commuters as customers, after 17:00 and before 19:00 Monday to Thursday.

It is up to you to identify your "undiscovered customer" and decide the best combination of circumstances to make first contact. To use the G.R.O.W.T.H.S. U.P. model most effectively, take into account all the environmental and personal factors you can and ensure first contact is a strong contact that will be seen or heard. Then the natural conversation will more easily flow to the next station on your journey of building "Rapport" with your "found customer".

With those general rules in mind let us examine specific situations where your research has identified the potential "undiscovered customer" and see how we could apply the model and the rules to maximise first contact.

Physical Identification

Let us begin with follow-up from a trade show where you perhaps met briefly with someone and/or got hold of their business card or came across them on a list of contributors.

In this instance you have made little or no personal contact with the person you are interested in but you do have considerable information available about them. Apart from checking Google, LinkedIn, Twitter and Facebook to see what you can find, you also know (as they were at the event you came across them) what they sell, how they see themselves, the kind of money they spent on their stand and possibly what it is they are looking for. Armed with this, and still using the model and rules we have just looked at, your first contact can be highly focused, meaning you can target the person and company with a contact that is respectful, positive and relevant to them.

That might be phone call where you can talk about the show, how impressed you were with their stand and how you noticed they have a need, which you would like to discuss helping them with. Alternatively, it might be an email; though be aware they will be sending many themselves after the show and receiving quite a few, so it should stand out.

Find a fact or piece of information that shows you are seriously interested in them and understand their needs. You might instead decide to make contact on social media. In which case the communication should be more precise and attract their attention in a positive, relaxed yet professional way. In all of these consider the rules above as to timing and channel.

The model works because you are not aggressively selling anything, just making contact because you believe they require help in an area you excel. Even if the contact goes no further, you have set up a possible future communication, introduced yourself and left them with a good feeling about you and your company. In the best case, the first contact will lead to a reply, which you can convert to the next station on your journey by building further rapport with a face-to-face meeting, a call, Skype, email or social media connection.

Let's take the following fictional example to illustrate one possibility.

You are a firm that makes quality promotional clothes for marketing and work purposes. You go to a local county business show not as a participant but just to see who is there. You walk around, talk to a few people, pick up the show brochure and as many cards as you can. While you are there, being clever, you take photos on your phone or tablet of some of the examples of marketing materials and promotional clothing people are using or displaying.

You come home and over the next week choose five possible "undiscovered customers" who look like they might need your product, either because they had no promotional clothing or because it is of a standard that is not nearly as good as yours. You check out the company using the method above. One company you decide to call as you actually met the person on the stand. You chose your time and day for maximum effect. In the call, you introduce yourself and remind the person where you had met and how impressed you were with the show and stand. You ask them about how successful it was for them and gently mention your company and what it does. All you need to say is that you think you could provide a great service and would love to pop round or meet up to show how. That's it. Be friendly, relaxed and respectful. Use the person's name, show you know about their company and how you could help.

The minimum return is that you will leave a good impression, which will stand you in good stead for the future. The maximum return is that the "undiscovered customer" becomes "found", agrees to follow-up and you move on to your next station on your journey, building "Rapport". Either way you have had a natural, focused, chat, which was your intent. No stress; job done.

If you felt an email was more appropriate, then again choose the time and day, personalise as above and briefly mention how impressed you were with them and would love to be of service. Tell them what you do and that you would love to call to discuss further. Ask them if you could call in a few days and leave your number. The worst result is no reply, and even that is good as you have established a positive, relaxed, point of contact. They might email and ask for more information, in which case you might consider calling with that information, or they might ask you to call. In any event your focused, natural, relaxed, approach, has worked and in most cases will lead on to the next station on your journey. Using social media, you can send a message to them on Facebook, similar to the email but make it more personal and focused and await the result.

Of courses there is a myriad of variations to each of these, but I hope this example gives you an idea of how the G.R.O.W.T.H.S. U.P. model can, at this stage, help you convert a first contact to a "found customer". Just use the relevant parts of S.M.I.L.E., a N.I.C.E. C.H.A.T. while staying on the PA.T.H .and being aware of any N.O.I.S.E., and the model will help you on you journey to converting the "undiscovered customer" into a "found" one where you can build that rapport and increase revenue.

The next scenario to look at is when you attended a networking event.

These events are both local and national. If you are new to them, I would suggest you try a local event first where you can attend by paying a fee or by being a visitor to see how they work. Some networking groups such as BNI make you join for a year, and there is a selection procedure, others like 4Networking give you a free first meeting, after which you pay for a series. The advantage to these groups is that everyone is there to promote their business and has contacts that might be useful to you. The disadvantage is that they are usually early morning breakfast meetings and you will have to stand up and present yourself for one or two minutes.

In any event, you have joined one and met several people and got their cards. See this group as a slow burn, not a quick fix. Build the relationships over time. Get them to know and trust you. So here, first contact is unlikely to lead quickly to the next station unless you have a specific product or service that is needed at that time by someone. In any event the method of connection here is meeting up.

So, when you have identified your potential "undiscovered customers" meet them at the group, talk to them, find out about them rather than pushing yourself on them, and then agree to meet up to chat further. This is where the G.R.O.W.T.H.S. U.P. model works best, allowing you to have that natural conversation, smiling and having a N.I.C.E. C.H.A.T., in a mutually interested and respectful environment. That is where – along with the meetings themselves – you can take first contacts onto the remainder of the journey, which will lead to revenue growth and new customers. These kinds of groups are perfect for small local businesses: from plumbers to estate agents and accountants to printers and reiki practitioners.

Now we look at what some find to be one of the hardest types of research follow-up where **you physically walk in to a company, be it a retail or service business.**

Your research has identified a business that has a physical presence and either, because you are unable to find a phone number or email or because you know their location, you decide to walk in and find out more about them. Remember the model, even here: you are just going to have a nice chat and leave the person feeling relaxed, curious and aware that you were genuinely interested in them.

This may be a casual walk-in because you just came across their premises and thought it might be of interest. Or it could be a retailer on your local high street or market that you have come across before, or know of, and want to convert into a "found customer".

As you walk in, they of course, will be expecting you to buy their product. Don't launch into a monologue of what you are and what you do. Use the model – have a natural conversation. Enquire about their product or service, express genuine interest and then, whether or not that product or service is something you need, gently introduce yourself and mention what you do or offer. At this stage that may be the end of it if you can see there is no interest. That is fine; you have made a contact, had the natural conversation and left a good impression.

On the other hand, your focused interest, respect and relaxed approach might stimulate curiosity in the person. They may ask you more questions. This is when you can begin to convert them to a "found customer" and move on to the next station. It may be inappropriate to go into detail there and then, so steer the chat into discussing when would be convenient to meet up or return and have a further chat. Don't pressure them; just offer it as a possibility. More than likely, as there is interest, they will give you a convenient slot. Then you can gently and easily move on in your journey with no hassle, no target or hard sell, just a nice chat with an engaged party. The model helps you achieve, effortlessly, the result you need.

The final physical research where you may want to create that connection with the "undiscovered customer" is an event that you organise.

This is likely to be local and, maybe because you want to tap into any local resources above and beyond what you have done research wise so far, you will probably advertise it locally in shops, businesses or in the local paper, or online on local websites. You will hire a room somewhere and ensure you have professional posters, business leaflets or material, as well as a way to communicate. This may be a straight talk in which you highlight your products, a presentation using PowerPoint or a video with a laptop and projector. Whichever method you use, it is essential, to maximise you time and cost, that you capture everyone who turns up.

You may charge an entry fee or not; that is up to you. Make sure there is a registration table. Have someone man it, if you can, and have a small simple form for people to fill out. The form should request as a minimum: their name, business, address, email, phone, web address and social media location. As an incentive to fill it out and register, maybe offer them a freebie such a pen or free leaflet or brochure as a good exchange.

Then whatever else happens you have a good source of "undiscovered customers" you can convert, if you wish, at a later date. This is your showcase. It is not a conversation, though even here the G.R.O.W.T.H.S. U.P. model will help. You need to project yourself as interesting, relevant, trustworthy and useful. Address the audience as equals; include them in your presentation. Make it natural and relaxed, not formal and stilted. Remember the models of communication we looked at before concerning voice, body language and words.

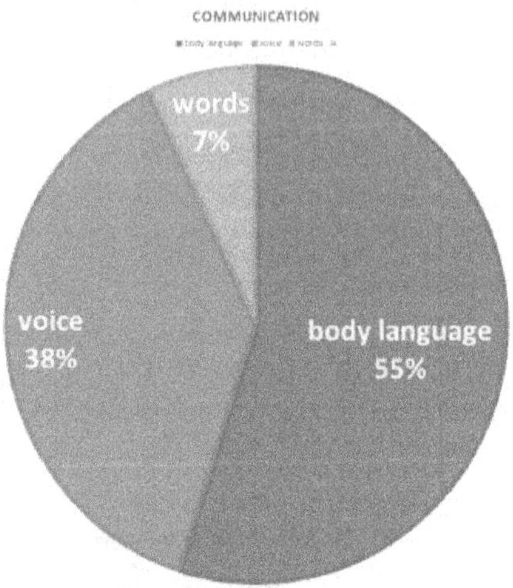

We will look at this in even more detail in our next station on our journey.

Establish a relaxed connection with your audience by telling a story and painting a picture – the skill that we looked at in staying on the right PA.T.H. S.M.I.L.E. relate to the audience as individuals, ask questions and encourage interaction. This relaxed, friendly approach will make far more of an impression than a stilted, aggressive sales pitch. The model will help you relax, be less stressed and deliver effectively.

Make sure you leave time at the end for people to come up to you and talk personally. If any of them expresses interest, make sure you get their card or make a note for further follow-up. This kind of event is excellent for harnessing local contacts – as long as you feel comfortable standing up in front of a group.

When you do follow-up, you will have already made the first contact and a good connection. This allows rapport to develop easily as they have already met you, feel safe with you and hopefully are interested in what you have to offer. I would follow up within one week of the event for maximum effect and, where possible, call the person to start the journey moving on.

Presentation skills are a workshop in themselves, so if you do have any specific questions, concerning how to present effectively, or would like more detail of my skills workshops on this subject, please do contact me at growthsup@gmail.com and I will be happy to help.

We have now looked at a variety of physical research possibilities and how to maximise them. It is now time to turn to digital research, what that might produce and how you might maximise contacts from the information you garner here.

First we will look at social media and how to follow-up from potential "undiscovered customers" that you have come across in this area.

People and companies use social media in a variety of ways; from the most informal to a means of marketing their product or service directly. When you come across a potential contact in this environment it is therefore important to look at how they present themselves to the world on platforms such as Facebook, LinkedIn, Twitter or any other social platforms. Once you have identified the potential contact, completed extra research into their company, product or service and are ready to contact them, you must consider that the style of contact must reflect how they present themselves on social media.

This environment is often more friendly, more targeted and more personal than a formal business environment. You must therefore consider tailoring your message to fit the environment and the image that the company or person projects. A relaxed message or post on Facebook might not work if you are sending a formal message on LinkedIn. Use the G.R.O.W.T.H.S. U.P. model and the skills it offers, such as telling a story, painting a picture, smiling, respecting the individual and focusing on them, to make sure that your message is attractive, relaxed, unique, captures the imagination and promises some form of response, where relevant. Unlike any email or a telephone call, the timing of this particular post or message is less important as people will access social media at any time and place convenient to them.

So, Facebook is a less formal than LinkedIn and your message or post should reflect that. Twitter, on the other hand, might be formal or relaxed. However, the important point to note is that you only have 140 characters to get your message across. So, whether it is a personal tweet or a general one, you need to make it stand out in the most precise and concise way to stimulate interest and get replies.

Even though the timing of social media is more flexible, for maximum impact I would recommend a response within 24 to 48 hours to any follow-up that you do get. You might find that the best way to initiate a contact on social media is to go on to the particular Facebook page of a company or a trade or networking group, and either post a message or like or share somebody else's. Whatever method you use, make sure – that using the G.R.O.W.T.H.S. U.P. model – your message is relaxed, respectful and positive and that you do follow up any contacts promptly.

Finally then, do your research, make sure that you understand the image and platform that somebody is using, and reply positively in a way that mirrors that image and conforms to the platform that they are using. This is where you are more likely to present a positive image, interest the potential customer and get a response.

Just a brief word on Google and Bing, the main search engines. They are an excellent tool for finding out the most you can about a person or company. Make sure you look at all sources of information that these search tools highlight and before contacting the company or person via social media or any other means, delve into any website or social media page that gives you more information. As we said before, 'time spent in reconnaissance is never wasted.'

Websites

As well as social media, the other area of research that might lead you to contact a potential customer is going direct to the company or person's website and contacting them there. Most websites have a contact page where you can send a message directly to the company. However, I recommend finding a phone number or a personal email and using those methods to contact an individual directly. Follow the suggestions for a telephone call or email exchange that we have looked at previously and use the model to make sure that your contact is relaxed, natural, friendly and focused.

Newspapers

One other source of information that is accessible in both physical and digital form is the newspaper. Nearly all national and local newspapers now have a website. These are a rich source of information for local and national companies and individuals that you may wish to contact. Use the newspaper website as your first port of call and then seek out more information, so you can get a complete picture before you contact the company or individual. The advantage to collecting information via a newspaper is that you might find out a lot more about the individual or company. For example, you might unearth information about a new product or service, growth in profits, hiring of new people, anniversaries or product launches – anything that you can use to be more relevant and more focused in your first contact. When you make contact it will be a natural conversation using the model and applying the skills to ensure that first contact can, where relevant, be converted into a meaningful exchange; a "found customer". You will then travel onward on your journey to the next station on the line, that of building "Rapport".

How you contact somebody that you have come across in a newspaper will follow all the rules you have looked at before; however, it is likely to be more formal than with someone you came across on social media, unless the information on our person or company shows them to operate in a relaxed and informal sector. Face-to-face is best, a phone call is good, Skype is excellent and an email or social media are your final alternatives.

Whatever you do in any of these first contacts, remember, you are not trying to sell anything; you are just making contact, showing interest, following the model and having a natural conversation. If all you do is make a good contact and leave a good impression then you have succeeded because that can always lead to future business. If you do get follow-up and there is interest shown, then you have a great chance of converting the "undiscovered customer" to a "found customer" and progress along your journey to the next station to one where you generate more revenue and increase your customer base. Whatever happens, it's a Win-Win. G.R.O.W.T.H.S. U.P. helps you in all the situations, maximises the environment, improves the contact, and offers success whatever the outcome.

So, there we have it; we have looked in detail at "Connect", the second station on our journey where you initiate first contact and convert the "undiscovered customer" to the "found customer". Either by just creating a good first impression or by applying the methods, platforms and communication skills we have used, move them on to the next station on your journey. That is the one where we build the rapport, have a meeting or meaningful social interplay and maximise the contacts to create a powerful exchange, which will be the station after. This will then hopefully lead to a transaction, increased revenue and a nurtured customer who will come back to us time after time and recommend us to their friends. As in the first station "Discover", so in this station "Connect", we have seen that the G.R.O.W.T.H.S. U.P. model works effectively. It helps you maximise your research, convert it into a first contact and in both physical and digital environments allows you, without stress, in a gentle and positive way, to move you and your customer on a journey to greater revenue and success.

14 STATION 3 RAPPORT

Now we have made first contact, discovered our customer and stimulated an interest to proceed further in which we can create a meaningful exchange – one that we hope will lead to a transaction – we have to accomplish the most important step. This is our most important station on our journey, where we build the rapport that all future success is based upon. The G.R.O.W.T.H.S. U.P. model and its tools of S.M.I.L.E., N.I.C.E. C.H.AT., RIGHT PA.T.H., and breaking through the N.O.I.S.E. combined with the focus, congruence and control of FCO^2, all come into play here to help you, in a relaxed, natural, way, build the rapport vital to the exchange and transaction.

The model will help, to gently create, without stress or manipulation, a safe bubble where you and your customer can exchange views and progress naturally to the next stage. Once you apply the model and its tools it is easy, natural and congruent with yourself, Here is how.

We are now at the stage of having connected with our customer and created sufficient interest that we have moved on in our journey to an actual meaningful meeting or social media exchange. This is where building rapport takes place, face-to-face preferably, or on the phone or online if not. The model gives you all the tools to create the safe bubble and have that natural conversation which will lead to a meeting of minds and a natural exchange. We have looked at the tools of S.M.I.L.E., N.I.C.E. C.H.A.T., the PA.T.H., N.O.I.S.E. and FCO^2; now we are going to apply them to developing that rapport and continuing your journey.

All of the tools, which hopefully you now understand and have started to use, come together here. We will begin with building rapport in a face-to-face meeting as this is the most critical and also the best environment to go forward.

Face-to-face meetings

From the moment your customer walks through the door of your establishment, whatever your product or service, you need to understand that everything you do, everything they see and hear, smell and touch will have either a negative or positive effect on how they react to you and how you build rapport. Every action and lack of action will either build a positive, safe environment in which to have your natural conversation or build barriers and reinforce the noise that customer might bring to the meeting. To use the model effectively and to get the most out of the tools, it is essential that the whole environment of your workplace works towards building a positive experience where a relaxed, natural conversation can take place in a secure, safe environment filled with good energy. In other words, to minimise the noise the customer brings to the encounter before you have even spoken.

So, before going into detail about how to build rapport using that smile, the nice chat and moving along the path, it is important to have just a few rules about how your customer should perceive your establishment from the moment they walk in the door. Then we can integrate an additional model of building rapport based on what your customer sees, hears and experiences in that environment.

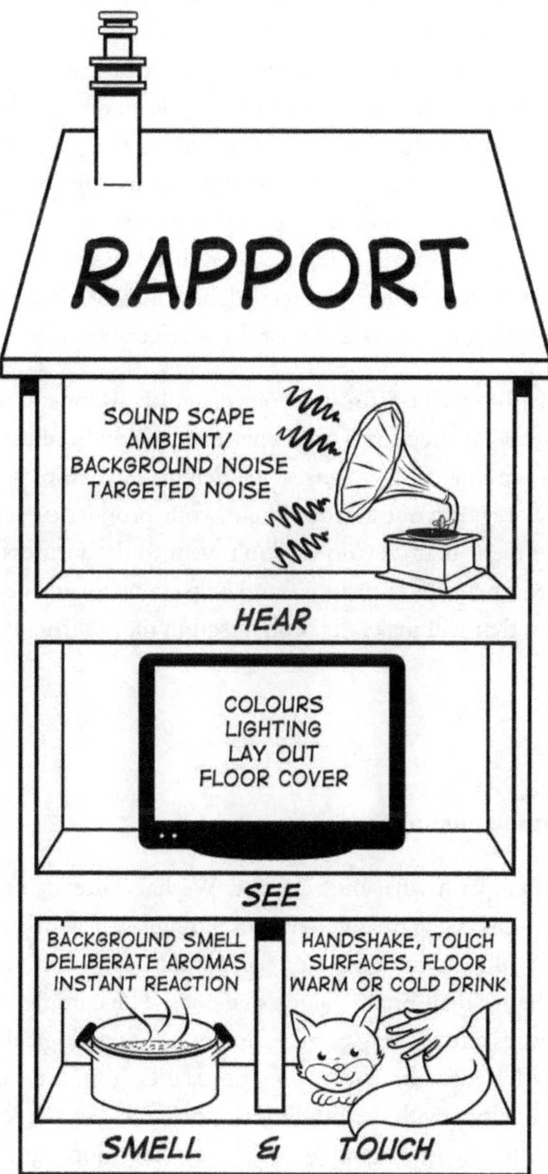
ELEMENTS IN THE ENVIRONMENT
AFFECTING RAPPORT IN 3 DIMENSIONS
RAPPORT
SOUND SCAPE
AMBIENT/
BACKGROUND NOISE
TARGETED NOISE
HEAR
COLOURS
LIGHTING
LAY OUT
FLOOR COVER
SEE
BACKGROUND SMELL
DELIBERATE AROMAS
INSTANT REACTION
HANDSHAKE, TOUCH
SURFACES, FLOOR
WARM OR COLD DRINK
SMELL & TOUCH

Physical environment

Let's begin with the physical environment they will experience once they enter your establishment. This is made up of the way your establishment looks from the outside (maybe something that you can't do a lot about), whether it is welcoming in the sense of colour, cleanliness and ease of access and how it looks when the person actually enters into the premises. As an example, if you serve customers who are disabled, having three steps outside your entrance will not create a positive message if somebody is in a wheelchair. If you are selling a service of well-being and calm, having the outside or inside of your offices painted bright yellow or bright red will create the wrong psychological impression for the service you offer.

So the customer has walked through your door. Let us look at what they see, what they hear, what they smell and what they touch; because whether you like it or not, each one of their senses will determine, before you have said a word, how they regard your establishment, your product or service and the kind of environment that they do or don't want to do business in. You can create an environment that is positive and helps your natural conversation or puts up barriers that will make that conversation more difficult.

Visual – what the customer sees

Let us begin then, with what they can see. We have already said that bright colours can be seen as aggressive and not caring, so if your business is one where you want the customer to be relaxed and positive, muted and pastel colours work better than bright, aggressive ones. The lighting you use is also important. Fluorescent lighting can create serious psychological problems for a lot of people. Indeed, some people get headaches from the almost unheard hum of old ones along with the brightness it provides. So think about having subdued or more friendly lighting, which sets the mood and directs your customer to where you want them to go. The combination of relaxed colours, natural light and subdued lighting will mean that your customer will enter into a world of relaxed calm as opposed to aggressive light.

This, of course, also extends to whether your floor is carpeted or has some other material on it. Again, if you're looking for a relaxed atmosphere, carpet or rugs, rather than harsh linoleum, will give a better impression and reduce the amount of noise in the establishment. While we are on the physical environment, also consider the space itself and whether your shelving display units, desks and open or closed floor plan provide the right atmosphere for the customer as they walk in the door. Whether it's an office where you wish to display your efficiency and professionalism, or a shop where you wish to display your goods in the best light, or even as a service provider where you wish to demonstrate a place of calm and positive energy, I hope you can see that the physical environment is vital to the picture you wish to paint and the bubble you wish to develop in which to have your natural conversation and build your rapport. There are many elements to the physical environment that you might be able to change or adapt to improve your chances in using the model and building the rapport.

Just one last consideration: how you brand your shop or premises is vital. Consistency of colour, logo and style ensures the customer sees the message you want them to see in harmony and without conflict. They feel right. Mix colours incorrectly or misplace branding, logos and style items and there will be an immediate visual disconnect between what you are about to say and what the customer sees.

Auditory – what the customer hears

So much for what you can see; now let's think about what the customer can hear. Of course this will depend on the current type of premises that you inhabit. An office will sound different to a store that sells furniture or a practitioner who offers relaxation technique. The point is that you have options as to the sounds your customer hears. These sounds divide into two sections. The first set of sounds is the background sounds. Just because they are background noises does not make them any less important. For example, an annoying hum from a machine or old lighting, banging from outside or someone fixing something, a radio playing loud music inappropriate to the location. Even members of staff arguing in the background can provide a negative first impression and build barriers to further communication and your attempt to have a natural conversation and use the model to build rapport.

So don't ignore your background sound environment. Most of it is under your control. You may decide that silence is the best way to greet your customer or you might decide that appropriate music or natural sounds work best depending on what product or service you are offering. Whatever you decide, make a conscious decision about what kind of background noise your customer will hear from the moment they walk in the door. Also be aware if you have noisy neighbours or live on a main road where there is a large amount of traffic noise: you might wish to soundproof your premises to reduce the stress that is inevitably caused by such background interference.

Now let's look at the second set of sounds which are the deliberate ones that you use to begin building that rapport. I am of course talking about how you and your staff address the customer from the moment they walk in. There is no casual comment. All communication that the customer hears in your premises will go towards building a positive or negative soundscape. This sound cape will affect how your customer perceives you and how positive or negative they are when they hear your message and listen to your natural conversation. So it is vital that this positive communication is correct from the start. You and your staff must ensure that any customer who walks in the door is greeted, according to our model, as a unique individual who is respected and is the focus of all our attention for the time they are with you. If you have a receptionist or other member of staff who will greet the customer first, they must be trained to treat each customer as the first customer. One of the biggest problems we face is being in a high volume business with a high footfall, such as a busy café, retail or office premises: staff can get swamped by the numbers and become tired, de-motivated and careless. That is why I say each customer is the first customer, even if it's the end of a busy day and everyone is tired.

So, not just what you say, but how you say it will determine how your customer sees you, hears you and perceives you. Make sure that from the moment they are greeted to the time they leave they are treated as you would wish to be – with respect, kindness, care and consideration. Do that and the G.R.O.W.T.H.S. U.P. model will work effectively, your natural conversation will flow easily and your rapport will build smoothly.

We will look at what you say and, more importantly, how you say it, in our three-dimensional model of building rapport a little bit later.

So, we have looked at what you can see and what you can hear, which of course are vitally important. It is also important not to neglect the areas of smell and touch.

Olifactory – what the customer smells

We begin by considering the power of smell. No, don't laugh. Smell is the most basic of senses and reacts mostly at a subconscious level, which is why it is so powerful in triggering memories and emotions. How many times have you smelt something that reminded you of an event in the past and immediately triggered that memory, good or bad? Because smell is a primitive sense and connects with that part of our brain it is hard to block out or filter. That is why, because of its powerful and immediate impact, it is essential that any smell the customer experiences when they walk in to your workplace is either neutral or positive.

Just imagine you sell bathroom products and as your customer walks in they smell blocked drains or wet clothing hanging in your office. Their immediate reaction will be negative and associative of an unclean environment. Now it will be so much harder to sell your product. That is why when selling your house, and it is a well-known trick, estate agents suggest that before someone comes to view it you should have fresh coffee or baking bread on the go. These two smells trigger feelings of comfort and security, are positive and help put the purchaser in the right frame of mind.

So, how in your environment can you use smell in a positive way to enhance your chances of having that natural conversation, preventing barriers and breaking through any noise? Well, if you have a shop that sells furniture then the smell of old antique wood or furniture polish conjures up positive feelings. In a clothes shop a smell of fresh linen would work. In an office, either neutral smells or coffee percolating would help, while if you were a practitioner of a well-being service, some aromatherapy oils or incense would create the ideal atmosphere. The point is that your customer will react to smell instantly and subconsciously without being able to filter it. As such, it will affect their mood, perception and interest before you say anything. Get it right and your natural conversation and the model will work smoothly. Get it wrong and you will have to work extra hard before you have even begun.

That is smell; now what about what the customer physically feels?

Kinaesthetic – what the customer physically touches

We are all affected to a lesser or greater degree by our physical interaction with the world. One of the most powerful yet often ignored interactions is that of touch. We know how wonderful it is to feel a mother's hug or a lover's kiss, but we often forget that other areas of touch affect us just as much and often totally subconsciously. So it is important that as well as having your premises looking right, sounding nice and smelling good, you also need to think about what your customer will touch.

Obviously the first thing to be aware of is cleanliness. If a customer enters your premises and it is full of dirt, cobwebs and greasy surfaces, once they touch any of them they will already be in a negative state. Just think about when you might have been to a café and the surfaces had not been well cleaned or the cups were dirty. Did you want to eat there or go back? So make sure, whatever your premises, that they are clean and any surfaces your customer might touch – from door handles to displays, from desks to products – are clean, especially if you have a washroom or equivalent that your customer might use. Make sure this is regularly cleaned and feels, looks and smells clean and hygienic. That's the basics. What else? Well, if you have a product that has a good feel to it, that is tactile like fur or feels cool, smooth or nice, make sure it is easily displayed so it can be touched and felt.

Some people are more kinaesthetic than others and like to touch and feel items. Older people might find touching an item or handling a book or file more satisfying than seeing something on a screen. The point is, it is your environment. Make sure it works for you and that people can touch, and what they touch gives off the right positive energy. On that one last point, there are several studies about what is known as "Priming". That is, setting up a state in someone's mind without them being consciously aware of it, to help them make decisions or act in a certain way. It has been proven that if you give a customer a warm drink, such as a coffee or tea, they will feel more positive and more disposed towards you than if you gave them a cold drink with ice. Don't believe me? Then look up the research.

[Bargh and Williams Yale University as quoted in an article]

Whether you take advantage of this or not is up to you. Certainly, offering a nice cup of tea or coffee in the right circumstances is not just good for touch but also for how people feel emotionally.

On that note, now we have brought into focus the physical environment and maximised its positivity, we are ready to build the rapport through our natural conversation, using our tools and a more detailed model, which you can see below.

Building personal rapport in 3 dimensions

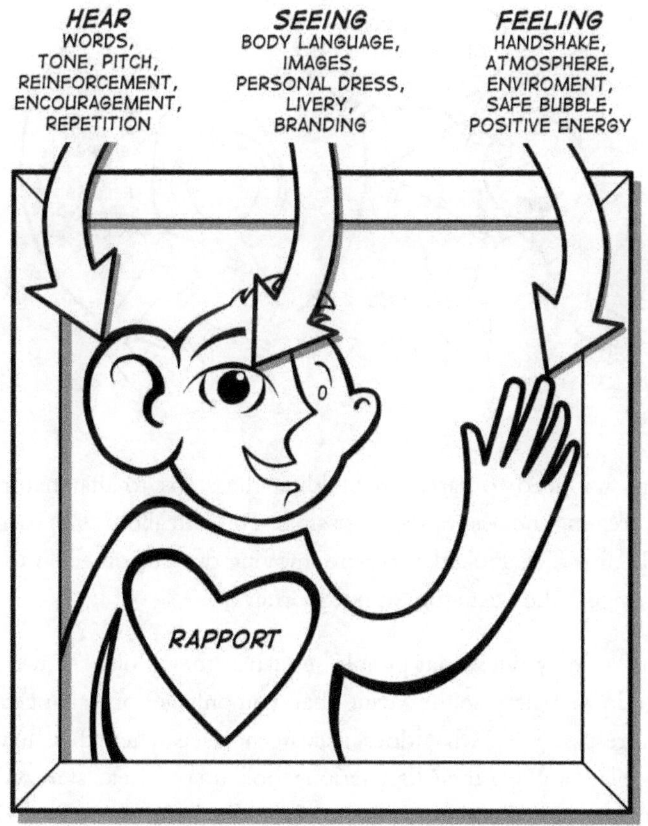

To build the rapport using our model, tools and its natural conversation, we need to be aware of how that conversation takes place. Once all the tools become unconscious competence, as we looked at before, you will find all this detail is integrated into your subconscious and, because the model is congruent with you, will flow automatically.

A cone of energy giving you all you need to have that natural conversation and which gives the customer a safe bubble where they feel the rapport and positive energy is the result of integrating these tools, the model and the journey – as seen in the diagram below.

CONE OF ENERGY

In the meantime, we need to carry on building the steps to that natural conversation by creating the best rapport possible. This will allow us to easily break through the noise we looked at before, moving our customer on to a worthwhile exchange – the next stop on our journey.

Let us begin with an easy one: what people see when they look at you and what should you do to maximise the saying that 'you only get one chance to make a first impression'? So what does a customer see when they have entered your premises and get their first serious look at you? Let's start with your personal appearance, then clothes and accessories before we move on to body language, which, as you remember, is 55% of the communication in our natural conversation. This will include personal space and an effective physical greeting.

Personal appearance

I am sure that you and your staff know that to dress appropriately and in the correct business clothes for your profession or role is vitally important. It is also essential you and your staff present the best appearance as to hair and make-up where relevant. The point is that your customer has expectations based on their noise, past experience and personal assumptions. If they are expecting a well-dressed person in a business suit and they get a person in flip-flops and jeans, they will already have put up barriers before you even start. The reverse is of course true. If you are running a pet shop, a polo shirt with your logo, sensible trousers and maybe an apron are more fitting than an expensive business suit. The point is that all the visual clues matter. So what you wear, how you brand your shop – as we have seen before – all count towards that positive or negative first impression.

Now we have the appearance right, what else will the customer see?

Well, here we can apply what we learnt in the chapter on S.M.I.L.E.

I need not repeat all of it, however to remind you of the relevant elements here is what the customer sees. Apply the G.R.O.W.T.H.S. U.P. model and the tools of:

Smiling: remember how powerful the smile is in creating a positive, safe environment.

Make eye contact. Again apply the rules we looked at in the chapter on SMILE. Take into account cultural and gender differences and establish a respectful focused, positive connection.

Also from SMILE, part of the **"L" was to Listen intently**. Your customer will notice if you are listening intently and focusing on them, so be a

lert and use the Active Listening technique from the start to indicate interest both visually and from an auditory perspective.

And finally from S.M.I.L.E., the other part of the "L" is for Looking closely. This will also signify interest, focus and awareness and make the customer feel they are the centre of attention and valued.

The tool, S.M.I.L.E., then, is applied in what the customer sees. By starting with a smile, making eye contact, you will later individualise the exchange, making sure that you looked closely, listened intently and led gently; and then engaged with your customer.

We have begun to create a visually positive environment and to this we must add what makes up 55% of any exchange – the remainder of our body language. How to apply this is as true from the start where the customer sees you for the first time, right through the exchange until the customer leaves. Again, there are no neutral postures. Your body language will either contribute to a positive, safe environment where the customer will feel relaxed and positive, or create a negative feeling in them, which will prohibit any natural conversation or good further connection.

Imagine you walk into a shop and the sales person ignores you, files her nails or crosses her arms and avoids eye contact. Or you walk into an office and the receptionist ignores you, and when you go to talk to her she puts her hand up to say, wait a minute. You are in a café and the waiter ignores your eye contact and then slams down your coffee or pastry and stomps off in a huff. In all these situations, without a word being said, you will feel angry, awkward and resentful. None of these emotions are likely to stimulate rapport or a good exchange.

Contrast that to walking into a shop and being greeted with a smile with the salesperson coming towards you open and positive, ready to help. The receptionist smiles warmly at you and makes good eye contact; the waiter walks positively towards you, looks at you and places the coffee on the table professionally then smiles and walks away. In these cases you feel much more positive and safe and therefore are open to further communication. So whatever the time of day, however busy you may be, each customer is the first customer and should be greeted visually, in a welcoming, focused, respectful way. Smile, make eye contact and move in their direction. Remember the rules of personal space we referred to before and do not crowd them.

We have now established the physical environment and visual landscape to maximise our chance at a positive natural conversation. The customer sees many good, strong, reinforcing, messages to make them feel safe, respected, and positive. Now we have to add to the mix the remaining 45% of the communications model: the words you use and the voice and its tone, pace and pitch.

In other words, in this first stage of building rapport, we now proceed to the auditory soundscape and ensure what the customer hears also offers strong, good messages, thus making them feel safe, individual, respected and ready to be helped. Just as visually there are no neutrals, everything the customer hears, whether in the environment (which we looked at before) or in what you say and how you say it, will contribute to creating either a positive or negative feeling and view of you. This will either help or hinder building the rapport and moving on to a concrete exchange.

In this auditory area you can apply the remainder of S.M.I.L.E., a well as elements of the N.I.C.E. C.H.A.T. and staying on the PA.T.H, as you stay natural, begin your exchange, highlight values, paint a picture and begin to tell a story. All of these are the tools we have looked at in previous chapters. Here you can apply them directly to building auditory rapport and then continue to use them through the following stages of our journey: "Exchange, Transaction And Nurture".

One fact you may not be aware of is that people listen at the speed they talk. This means that to have the best natural conversation you can, paying attention to the speed of your customer's speech and adjusting to it will greatly help build rapport.

Let me explain further. If you are one of those people who tend to talk fast or very fast, then there is no problem if you are talking to someone similar to you as they will match your speed and listen and hear what you say easily. However, if your customer is one of those who talks more slowly, likes to pause a lot, and consider what they say before saying it, your speaking fast will be almost impossible for them to process.

The result is that after a minute the part of the brain that processes auditory responses will overload. All they will hear is a hum and find it very difficult to understand you. Indeed they will feel uncomfortable and confused. That's not a good way to begin building rapport or that natural conversation. Try this out for yourself. Repeat out loud one word like, 'interpret' very fast twenty or so times and you will find it very quickly loses all meaning. This is the effect a fast talker has on a slow, more deliberate listener. Remember, we listen at the speed we talk.

The other extreme is also true. If you are the kind of person who talks deliberately with many pauses, allowing time to consider, and are talking to someone who talks and therefore listens quickly, they will begin to get frustrated with the slow pace and their subconscious thought will not be not what you are saying, but 'oh, just get a move on.' This is also not a good way to build rapport or have that natural conversation the G.R.O.W.T.H.S. U.P. model calls for. So listen to your customer and pay attention to the speed of delivery. If you are a fast or slow talker, try to modify it to match them. They will hear clearer, understand better and feel safer and more relaxed. That is building rapport.

We have also looked previously at using the right kind of language, and I refer you back to the visual, auditory and kinaesthetic language we discussed in the chapter on staying on the right PA.T.H. Where possible, begin to attune yourself to your customer's speech patterns and reflect them back. It may sound difficult and artificial, but with practice I assure you it becomes second nature and will greatly enhance your success of building rapport and having that natural conversation.

So, we have the speed right and the words we use reflect back our customer's preferences. We are well on the way to begin building that rapport through the natural conversation that our customer hears. We are not finished yet though. What they hear will also be affected by your voice and how you use it. Your tone and pitch, and how you encourage and support in your voice, repeat back information and respond to clarify and reinforce the connection – even your accent – will all affect positively or negatively what the customer hears, the impression they form and the level of rapport you can build.

Let us begin here with the tone, pitch and accent of your voice. We have already discussed the pace.

First the tone: this is where you connect with your customer at a subconscious level. To build rapport and begin that natural conversation make sure your tone is warm and positive. Make sure that any inflection is strong and resonant. By smiling as you talk your tone will sound even friendlier and more welcoming. To check whether your tone works, practice it with a friend or colleague. Try out different tones and see the reaction you get. The warm, positive, energised tone will make you and your customer feel the safest and the most relaxed.

Now what about pitch? We all have it; some people talk with a high, squeaky pitch, others with a deep, low, bass pitch. First, be aware of your voice and how you sound to others, not how you sound to yourself. If you have never tried it, record yourself and play it back. I bet you sound different to how you thought you sounded in your head. That is because the brain has a filter that reduces the strength of your voice when you are hearing it. The human ear processes different pitches differently. A high pitch is generally not conducive to building rapport as it triggers subconscious images of a whiner or child, which is not good for building confidence or connection. On the other hand, a lower pitch resonates more effectively with the human ear and summons up images of trust, reliability and professionalism. So whatever your natural pitch, practice having it in the middle to low range for best results in creating rapport with your customer.

Finally there is accent. Like pitch, we all have one. When we live and work in a specific area or with a defined group of people, we probably don't notice or even think we have an accent. As everyone sounds similar, the brain analyses the sounds as familiar and therefore easy to understand and feel comfortable with. Some of us, and some regions, have stronger local accents than others. In the UK, think of a strong Glaswegian accent being understood by a Londoner or a cockney being understood by someone from Leeds. In the USA, a Brooklyn resident speaking to a person from the southern states might find equal problems. The point is, if you have to deal with people not in your own group or not from your own area, be aware that your accent, though fine to you, might not be understood by others. In fact, it might act as a barrier to communication. If you do have a strong regional accent, then moderate it when talking to someone from another area or group. Speak slower and enunciate words more. Some accents seem to encourage swallowing words; for instance, Estuary English or some of the Norfolk dialects.

No accent is right or wrong. We have moved on from the days when BBC received pronunciation was considered correct. Just be aware that accent can aid or be a barrier to communication. As an example, some gentle Scottish accents are considered best for advertising as they invoke trust. Posh, clipped accents suggest class even if it's not true and some street accents alienate others.

Just a final comment on words. We have talked about VAK language and matching your customer's visual, auditory and kinaesthetic preferences in our chapter on PA,T,H. I just wish to include here one warning. Every group, professional or social, tends to use language and phrases, terms and abbreviations, and jargon particular to that group. Professional groups use it to stay exclusive and as a shortcut to understanding. Social groups use it for inclusion, exclusivity and for their members to feel in and part of a greater whole. If you know any military personnel then ask them about acronyms. Or ask a doctor or lawyer about their professional language. Again, if you are talking to someone not in your profession or trade, make an effort to avoid jargon and "in" language as it may alienate them and make them feel too embarrassed to ask you to explain.

So we have the environment right and our customer sees and hears us in a positive light. All we need to do now, to complete the communication in our favour, is to ensure that smell and touch compliment the good impression we have already created.

Regarding smell, I have mentioned before how it is the most primitive of senses and instantly conjures up emotions and memories. So, in your personal environment, make sure you and your staff have a neutral or positive odour. In other words, that they wash and use deodorant in the summer. (You might be surprised how many don't!) If you and they wear perfume or cologne, make sure that it is not too pungent and is subtle rather than aggressive as that might trigger a wrong feeling in some customers.

Finally, touch. In that first contact face-to-face, how you communicate by touch will also send out a negative or positive message. In the Western world a handshake is the normal way to greet someone. Obviously, you don't shake hands with a customer coming in to the store for the first time. However, if you have a specific appointment or know the person, a handshake is often expected. Even this is not as straightforward as you might think. People have expectations of how a handshake should feel. Too strong and it can feel dominating and aggressive. Too weak and it can conjure up images of weakness and insincerity. So be aware when you do shake hands that the other person has expectations. I would make the handshake strong but not overpowering and aim for a stronger grasp with men rather than women.

There are infinite variations. Politicians like the handshake with the freehand placed on the upper arm, for example. Different cultures shake hands differently: the Germans have more up and down shakes than the British for example. I do not intend to list them all here, but if you are really interested there is plenty of information about the differences on the internet to look at. Just be aware that your handshake is important; there is an expectation and don't treat it casually. This, combined with eye contact and personal space, when done correctly, creates exactly the image and feeling of safety and focus that is ideal for that natural conversation to begin.

One final point, handshakes are not the norm in Eastern cultures. Here bowing and offering business cards has a different rhythm and routine. If you are going to be dealing with customers from an Asian culture, please be aware there are many differences and you should do your research thoroughly so as not to offend them.

Feeling

All of these elements contribute to how your customer feels. Get them right and you create a safe bubble; a positive, respectful, calm, environment that places the customer in a wonderful, positively energised, secure, comfortable place in which to have that natural conversation and easily build that rapport. Fail to create that environment and the customer will feel ill at ease, fearful, confused, angry or scared; and you will find the noise generated drowns out any attempt to have that positive conversation and any feeling of rapport.

The digital and social media environment

So we have begun the process of building rapport in the physical environment. Now we must turn to the phone call and then social media and emails. These present more challenging environments for building that rapport as we have lost a major part of our communication.

First let us consider phone calls. Even though these are not as good as face-to-face meetings to build rapport as we have lost 55% of our communications, we can still maximise them to create a positive conversation in a focused and supportive environment. Remember in the chapter on SMILE, we met "LERT" and an **"L"** was to **Listen intently**. Your customer will notice if you are listening intently and focusing on them, so be a

"Lert" and use the Active Listening Response Technique from the start.

Let's look at this in more detail while reminding ourselves of what we said before.

To be like "Lert" all you have to is: close your eyes, slow your breathing so it is deeper, physically listen (it's an act of will), concentrate all your mind on listening and ignore outside stimuli. Be like a sniper and focus only on the person you are in front of or talking to. Filter out any noise or distraction in your own environment and focus totally on the person on the other end of the phone.

A.LE.R.T. means you can filter outside distraction at their end too, allowing you to receive a more complete mental picture. You will be able to feel the emotional state of the person on the phone by more easily assessing the background and context they are talking in. This will allow you to answer more quickly and more accurately and help you resolve problems more effectively.

So what are you tuning in on by being a "Lert"? Well, first their breathing: is it hurried or relaxed; are they anxious or calm? Knowing this will help you use the right words to help them get to the calm, positive state you want to build that rapport. Is there a lot of background noise there that might distract them: for example, kids crying, dogs barking, travel tannoy announcements, people talking loudly?

Being aware of anything that distracts them from focusing on you will help you be aware of it, acknowledge it in a positive and supportive way and deal with it. This will help the customer to focus on you and on the rapport you wish to build.

Then, what about their tone? Is it warm and interested or cold and detached?

Are the words they are using V A or K? What is their pace – slow or fast and can you match it? By applying Active Listening Response Technique and really focusing on your customer, even with 55% of the communication gone, you can still understand and empathise with them, their state and environment. This will allow you to frame the natural conversation more specifically. You will be able to acknowledge any reserve or problems they may have and create a better, safer, bubble from which to build the rapport. This will allow you more easily and in a focused, congruent way to move the conversation on to either an exchange on the phone or a face-to-face meeting.

By being A-LERT you will be able to ask relevant and meaningful questions and reply to the responses precisely and powerfully.

So being A-LERT and applying **A**ctive **L**ist**e**ning **R**esponse **T**echnique will allow you to listen intently, have a natural and powerful meaningful conversation and help you S.M.I.L.E. even more effectively.

By the way, research has shown that the old adage 'smile on the phone, people can hear your smile' really works as when you smile, your voice changes as well as your internal state, which provides a more positive, energised and happy voice, tone and energy.

We now turn to the digital environment of social media and then the last and most challenging one – email.

I am going to start with the easiest one, which is Skype.

Skype has many advantages: it is free[where stated before]; you can speak to many at the same time and share documents and desktops. It is as close to a face-to-face as you can come without actually being in the room. As such, because you are dealing with virtually all the communications model, the rules of the face-to-face meeting apply.

Just one caveat: you are not in the room with someone and as such the emotional content is not there in the same way. Even though they can see and hear you, they can't touch, smell or feel you. This means you need to focus even more on what you do see and what you hear, making up for that shortfall. So apply a mixture of the techniques from the face-to-face to the **A**ctive **L**ist**e**ning **R**esponse **T**echnique, where they fit, and you will be able to build a positive response and have a more natural conversation.

Smiling is very important here; genuine smiles with your eyes and mouth, as false ones will trigger suspicion. You need to radiate even more positive energy to compensate for them not actually feeling, touching or smelling you. That said, Skype is a great way to start the process of building rapport. If you can convert it into a real face-to-face, geography and time zones withstanding, then you should. If not, maximise your Skype time; focus on the customer and utilise all of the techniques you have so far learnt, the tools given to you and the G.R.O.W.T.H.S. U.P. model's application.

Social media

Now the easy one is out of the way, we need to look at how possible it is to build rapport using social media. Twitter cannot build rapport; it is only 140 characters and any tweets should be steered as quickly as possible to other social media, a call or meeting. That said, LinkedIn is a useful, professional environment to begin the process, although it seems to me to be a bit too cold, clinical and detached to really build the rapport. Here, I would, after one or two messages, move the conversation, if possible, to a call, or face-to-face, to really build the rapport. If that is not possible, then maybe move to email, or if continuing the LinkedIn contact, direct them to your website and maybe move them on from there.

Facebook is still probably the easiest, most relaxed and personal way to build rapport and have that natural conversation on social media. You have choices of mixing the contact between an instant message, a post, a like, or sharing material. You can download their content or post yours. As we mentioned before, mirror the level of formality, language and visuals to make the customer feel relaxed, safe and interested. When possible, if possible, see if you can replace the chat into a call, Skype session or face-to-face meeting maybe by contacting them first via your website or directly.

As we said previously, use the G.R.O.W.T.H.S. U.P. model and the skills it offers, such as telling a story, painting a picture, smiling, respecting the individual and focusing on them, to make sure that your message is attractive, relaxed, unique, captures the imagination and promises some form of response, where relevant. Unlike any email or a telephone call, the timing of this particular post or message is less important as people will access social media at any time and place convenient to them.

Finally we come to email. Though very convenient and accessible, emails are difficult and dangerous if handled incorrectly. Remember, in emails you are only dealing with 7% of the message. You have lost most of it; the emotion, the voice, the body language, the energy. So you are reliant just on words. Some words of warning: first, never send an email without reviewing it and taking a few seconds to rethink it. Because there are no emotions in emails they need to be neutral or very clear, utilising unambiguous and positive language. If the person receiving it is in a negative state or bad mood, then an email you might think was nice and positive can be taken as negative and aggressive and you will not have any more communication.

An example. I am a good and appreciated employee. I feel confident that I have worked well and am appreciated and my boss sends me an email that says, 'Bruce, you should take a holiday.' As I am in a positive frame of mind, I see this as recognition of my hard work and of my boss looking out for me. Now, contrast this with a worker who feels under pressure, insecure and undervalued; maybe even worried about the security of their role. They receive the same email. What do you think goes through their mind, or yours? Is he trying to get rid of me, what are they really saying, is he firing me?

The point is that the receiver's state will determine the way the message is received unless it is unambiguous, clear, focused, and the language is very precise in what it is trying to communicate. That is why building rapport via email is so hard because you are only working with 7% of the model. Also, its convenience makes it dangerous. It is too easy to just send off an email without thinking. That is why I say, always review it first and check if it really says what you want it to.

Finally, ensure in an email, where you are trying to build rapport and have a natural conversation, that you use the person's name and title correctly and don't misspell it. Nothing is more annoying. Also, take in to account when the best time is to send the email for maximum effect as most busy people have many emails to review. I know I was getting sixty a day in one, not so busy office. So don't send an email as soon as your customer comes back from a trip, for example, as they probably have several hundred to plough through and won't be best disposed to answer yours.

Finally, try and convert the email as soon as possible into a telephone call, a Skype call or a face-to-face meeting to really start to build the rapport and have a meaningful and natural conversation.

So there we have it; we have completed the first stage of building the rapport, taking into account the physical, personal and digital environment. Now it is time to take all that hard work onto the next station on our journey – "Exchange", where we will develop the relationship further and make our natural conversation even more powerful and meaningful.

15 STATION 4 EXCHANGE

We have made the connection, begun to build the rapport and now we must transition that hard work into a meaningful exchange. The target, as always with the G.R.O.W.T.H.S. U.P. model, is that natural conversation, so at this station we will explore how to continue the model, tools and the process to convert our connection and rapport into having a complete exchange. Unlike in sales processes and scripts, the objective of this station and the exchange is NOT completing a sale or having the customer ready to buy. The exchange is about leaving the customer feeling happy, well served, informed and satisfied – all with our natural conversation and without any need to become stressed about having to close or sell as a measure of success.

The "found customer" will at this stage be converted into one of two below, both the result of a successful, complete exchange. The first is the "Desirous buying customer" who will go on to the next station on our journey of "Transaction". The other is the "Happy but unbuying customer", who will leave satisfied, happy, prepared to consider you for a future purchase or service, and ready to move to the final stage of our journey "Nurture" and become a future customer. Both exchanges are deemed complete and successful. By having your natural conversation and giving the customer a great experience in a safe, secure, positive and relaxed atmosphere, they will leave feeling good about you and themselves. This will be either with a desire to purchase, ready to buy and tell others; or without a desire to purchase now, yet still ready to consider future transactions and happy to let others know about you. In either instance, your long-term reputation is enhanced and potential increased. That is a complete and successful exchange.

Here's how we get there using our tools and model and applying them on our journey.

This is where elements of all of our tools come into play. The S.M.I.L.E., N.I.C.E. C.H.A.T., staying on the PA.T.H., hopefully having already broken through the N.O.I.S.E., and utilising FCO2 to enhance our natural conversation and customer experience.

As before, we will divide this section into two aspects: the physical and the digital environment.

The physical environment

We have built the initial rapport, welcomed the customer and are now ready to begin our natural conversation in earnest.

Let us start with our S.M.I.L.E

As we discussed in the previous chapter, we have already greeted our customer with a smile knowing the benefits that accrue from that, and of course we will continue to smile naturally during this phase. Let us add to that the "I" for individualise, where here in our natural conversation, you empathise with your customer – as an equal, happy to help and guide, not control or fear. This positive, relaxed mindset engendered by the G.R.O.W.T.H.S. U.P. model means you will have a joyous, successful encounter whatever the exchange. This will happen naturally and positively.

So focus on the person and the moment. By having your focus on the customer and having that individual conversation with someone you want to understand and help, you can avoid the distraction of outside pressures or rigid frameworks or scripts. Go with the flow and let your natural energy and conversation embrace both of you in a generous, giving and positive atmosphere.

We have understood that we must Listen intently. Let us add the other "L"s in S.M.I.L.E: first "Looking closely", reminding you to focus, solely on the person you are engaging with at that moment, in that space. You should place all your energy on looking at them, engaging with them, and free from distractions build a natural conversation in an atmosphere that is friendly relaxed and positive. The final "L" here, as you will recall, is to "Lead gently". This is to remind you that unlike the aggressive, dominating sales culture where you are there to win a war, qualify objections and force a close (all aggressive leading techniques), in the G.R.O.W.T.H.S. U.P. model we are there solely to have a genuine relaxed conversation and at this stage a complete exchange. That is done, not by short-term aggressive manipulative Win-Lose behaviour, but by engaging in a gentle process of leading, that will end up as a Win-Win for both of you; not just now but in the future too. The atmosphere you should create, I would suggest, is summed up perfectly in the quote below.

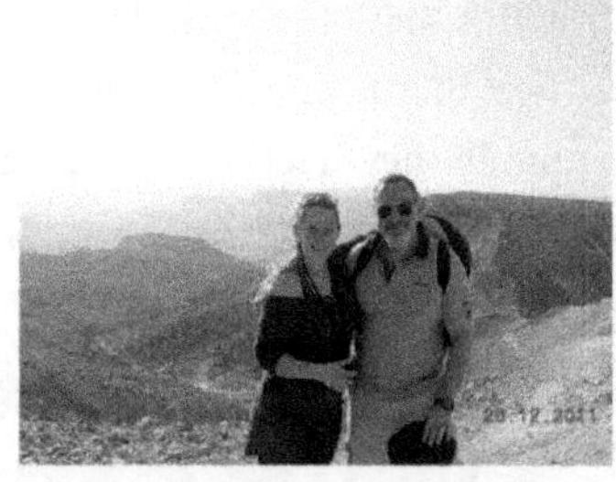

Don't walk in front of me ; I may not follow. Don't walk behind me; I may not lead. Just Walk beside me and be my friend -Albert Camus

So, don't glance, hear without understanding or lead aggressively; that's for old-style sales not our natural approach. G.R.O.W.T.H.S. U.P. takes you down the path of gentle, moral, congruent and joyful success. Embrace it and feel your energy flow. Finally from S.M.I.L.E., make sure you Engage with your customer by having a natural, flowing conversation that is grounded in the moment, without distraction, fear or resistance.

That is the emotional sound and vision-scape you want to project: the safe, secure bubble extending through this part of the journey, putting the customer in the most relaxed, open and positive frame of mind and heart, so they listen to you and engage freely in your natural conversation. Let us take this deeper using our other tools.

The conversation at this stage should apply the rule that you have two ears and one mouth, so listen twice as much as you talk. To have our natural conversation, move forward and transition to the exchange. Having built the initial rapport, you now need to understand what the customer needs and how you can help them fulfil it.

To do this we do not pressure or use aggressive, manipulative sales techniques. Instead we maintain the safe, relaxed, open atmosphere and use our open questions to take the conversation further. By the way, at this stage, have you offered the customer a cup of coffee or tea? Remember warm drinks can make the customer warm more to you. (Unless it's a boiling hot day of course and then water or a cold drink should be offered.) Have you given your customer a seat and started showing them any literature, products or presentations you might have? This is the stage where all of this will come together. Our tools and our model will show the way as follows.

The N.I.C.E. tool, as you recall, offers the framework of being natural, treating your customer as an individual, being clear in your words and in how you relate to them; and most importantly for this station, reminds you that your goal is an exchange, no more no less. For that exchange to now take place, we need to know what the customer thinks they need or want, clarify it, maybe help them decide if they are unclear or unsure, and move them forward with understanding, knowledge and focus to the exchange. Let me remind you of what Henry Ford said: 'If I had asked customers what they wanted they would have said a faster horse.'

The tool that applies most here is of course the C.H.A. of C.H.A.T.

For it is here that we apply **the first letter in C.H.A.T. the "C" which stands for clarifying needs**. As you recall, we are looking to ascertain why the customer is here and/or why they are talking to you specifically.

How do we do this in the most natural and relaxed way? Rather than use stilted scripts or aggressive, manipulative questioning as advocated in some sales techniques, the G.R.O.W.T.H.S. U.P. model utilises the natural flow of dialogue to gain the answers to help you serve your customer best. We use open questions, which is a more relaxed way of eliciting information. These consist of the five "Ws" – who, what, when, where, why, and how. Where appropriate, I would in certain circumstances add a sixth "W" – which. The other gain, using this model, is that it avoids the worst retail question used by so many, which is: 'Can I help you?' This is a closed question, not an open one and risks the answer 'No', which prevents any natural conversation proceeding. Using the six "Ws" we avoid this and obtain the information we need to help the customer make the best choice.

By using this natural formula in a different order, you can genuinely tap into the customers' needs, as illustrated in the diagram below. The final question "How", seen here for completeness, belongs to our next station on our journey, "Transaction".

These open questions should be asked slowly and in a relaxed, interested and focused manner. You are not interrogating your customer; you are treating them with respect and interest, helping to understand their needs better so you can make sure you can serve them best.

This method, linked to the S.M.I.L.E. and N.I.C.E. has guided you naturally and in a relaxed way to clarify the customer's needs, allowing you to focus clearly on that. You have avoided the use of scripts or other artificial sales gimmicks and still acquired the information you need naturally and in a positive collaborative atmosphere. To facilitate the exchange, whether or not there is a product or service you can provide to the customer, it is also important to include the second letter in C.H.A.T. – **the "H" which stands for highlighting value.**

As you recall, value is defined as 'The regard that something is held to deserve; the importance, worth, or usefulness of something.' So once you have established what if anything the customer is considering, ensure you highlight the value by including a value proposition statement. The ideal value proposition is concise and appeals to the customer's strongest decision-making impulses. It should be clear, stated in a few words only, explain the uniqueness of the product or service and the benefit the customer will gain. For example: if you had a bakery your statement might be: 'Our bread is always fresh. Guaranteed every day.' Or 'Walmart is the leader in low prices and huge selection.' Or 'Google is the "search engine of the world."'

Remember that value and a customer's decision-making is subjective and based on assumptions, desires, previous experience and perception of the product and environment. It is also to do with common rules we buy into, but which really don't exist. For example, the value of money is only what we accept it to be – not its intrinsic value. The value of stocks and shares is in the end subjective. The price of a product rarely reflects the cost of production. For example, an expensive watch or bag, or luxury item, is priced because of its name or appeal, not its cost to produce. At the other end of the spectrum, a shirt costing £2 in a supermarket: do we consider how it could have been made that cheaply and what manufacturing techniques might have been used to get that price?

With that in mind, consider that here we are looking at ensuring that your customer has a reason to consider purchasing the product or service from you. They are looking for exactly what you would look for, which is good value. So, why not start with what would you want to know about the service or product, talk about that benefit and see if that resonates with your customer? If that benefit resonates with your customer then continue along this path, amplifying the detail, always asking the customer what they think so you maintain focus, receive feedback and talk with them – not to them. Then you can focus on the relevant value to the customer. There is no point stressing the value of, say, a washing machine running quietly if the person actually has a priority for the size of load and that is what they consider good value.

Naturally what then follows in your relaxed chat is why it is worthwhile to that person and what will they get out of it. Remember this is a N.I.C.E. C.H.A.T. with an individual, unique person whom you wish to serve, respect and help. Their value is personal and so your questions and responses should not be highlighting what you wish to push but what they need for the product or service to **add value** to their life and be **of value** to purchase. Concentrate on that, gently and respectfully, and your customer will move through the exchange to a transaction that is revenue enhancing.

The conversation should then naturally flow into whether this product or service has the features they need. Remember, you are not selling anything; you are merely finding out if this product or service suits your customer, a bit like a well-fitting glove or nice woolly sweater. If they feel good about the product or service at this stage because the fit is there, then you can easily illustrate the advantages that are relevant to them and the value will be clear.

It is at this stage that the price, if not already obvious, should be highlighted in a relaxed, positive manner. You are happy and congruent with the value and therefore are not embarrassed about it, and have agreed it with your customer. This is done in a natural way as part of the conversation about value. Your customer will be happy to accept it if the value is clear, and agree. If the price is not accepted first time, then, if relevant, negotiate the best price, or if there is no agreement on price, move on gently and positively without fear or awkwardness as below.

However, if the product or service is not a good fit or does not suit, that is also OK because your target is the natural conversation leading to a complete exchange, not the sale. You have demonstrated value by your approach, concern and focus, and by your respectful treatment of them as an individual.

You have found that out in a relaxed way and can either offer another product or service that will fit, or more importantly, if you don't have one, don't worry.

Thank them for their time and if you can point them in the right direction, even if it's to a competitor, do so. You will lose nothing by this. The customer will remember your honesty and genuine help and will come back to you for something else. More than that, because this honesty and naturalness is so unusual they will tell their friends and colleagues. Your reputation will be enhanced and you will get more customers and exposure. **This has led you to the second of our successful exchanges – "The happy but unbuying customer."**

So, not selling – just chatting and being honest – will reward you and you will feel good as well. You have highlighted your value and even though the product or service might not have been the right fit, your value as an honest, trustworthy person has been established. You have sown a seed that can bring immense value in the future. It is the future that is the goal, building your reputation and brand forward, adding value with every N.I.C.E. C.H.A.T. whatever the outcome.

Having highlighted value, we can now move smoothly on to the next letter in C.H.A.T. – **the "A" which stands for "Agree an exchange"** – that being whichever of the two exchanges is the natural consequence of your conversation so far: "the desirous buying customer" ready to move to "Transaction" or "the happy unbuying customer" ready to move to "Nurture".

This is relatively simple, yet in selling people get stressed, find this hard and avoid it. In old-style sales techniques the exchange is associated with targets, qualifying the objections, closing the deal and asking for money; all questions and requests a lot of even professional salespeople hate and fear. Because they fear this it often colours their whole discussion and some even forget or avoid asking for the exchange because they are so stressed out and sure they will fail. What a waste of effort and mind-sapping, energy draining activity.

In contrast, the G.R.O.W.T.H.S. U.P. model is about energising and relaxing you by having a naturally flowing conversation – your N.I.C.E. C.H.A.T. Remember you are not selling anything. Your target is your conversation, whatever the outcome, and an exchange is always possible without pressure or stress. That will make it happen. At this stage, you have clarified your customer's need and highlighted the values. Purchase or not, your customer wants to proceed with an exchange.

In fact, your customer needs it. Both sides want a conclusion. Your natural chat will ensure that conclusion is Win-Win. As it has been a natural, relaxed conversation rather than a high-pressure sales technique, both of you are relaxed. The customer wants what you are offering and you are happy to offer it to them. This might be an actual purchase or transaction or it might be the offering of value, as discussed before, of an honest, trusted exchange that will leave them feeling positive, happy and relaxed.

That is the value you have offered: the exchange that has taken place. This means you will have a Win-Win exchange, which will set the scene for future success. The conclusion of the exchange, needed to satisfy both you and the customer, is either tying up the transaction (which we will look at next) or thanking the customer for their time. You may have offered another solution, even if it involves a competitor; or just ensured they have had enough time and space to finish chatting to you without feeling rushed or pressured into buying. You have given them all the time they need and they leave happy and satisfied because even without a purchase both sides have exchanged value, as we discovered before.

Both sides feel good, relaxed, happy and satisfied. That means both sides can smile and the relationship – built on trust and natural flow – has reached a natural conclusion. This means that both sides have built bridges for more exchanges IN the future – a Win-Win.

We will look at the last letter in C.H.A.T. when we come to our next station, "Transaction".

So to ensure our exchange takes place after making the connection, building rapport, asking questions and highlighting value, we can bring our other tool into play; that of being on the right PA.T.H. Using this tool, as you remember, to paint a picture, tell a story and continue to have that conversation.

We paint the picture better, in this section of natural conversation leading to an exchange, where we utilise NLP VAK to use words more relevant to that person's modality or style of thinking and communication. The chapter on PA.T.H. went into great detail on this and I won't repeat it here.

Once we have used the relevant language to paint that picture, we can enhance this section and our natural conversation by using one of the best methods to continue the building of rapport and the path to exchange – that of telling a story.

Storytelling, as you know, is one of the oldest human skills, and we all love a good story. Most of us are brought up on stories when as children our parents would read us bedtime stories, or we would hear teachers or friends telling them. Stories, if told naturally and honestly, engage the listener and personalise you and a product or service that might seem to the customer cold or distant. In this section, leading to our exchange, highlight your product or service by telling a story that relates them to your customer's experience, concerns or interest.

For example, if the customer is looking for an insurance quote from you and had a bad experience with being overcharged, a story where you helped a customer and in similar circumstances would put them at ease and show shared values. Or, if the customer was looking to buy a present for their partner and couldn't decide between several products, maybe a story of how you assisted a similar customer and how they made their choice or perceived their value, might help.

The point is, relate the current customer need and desire for exchange to a past relevant, genuine, story that sets the scene for a decision and an exchange in a relaxed, friendly and focused manner. You will enjoy telling the story, the customer the experience, and the exchange will follow more easily and more naturally.

I remind you, storytelling also stimulates a powerful neurological response. According to neuroeconomist Paul Zak, research suggests our brains produce the stress hormone cortisol, which we have already identified, during tense moments in a story. This allows us to pay attention and focus, while a part of the story that has sweet or gentle parts to it stimulates the release of oxytocin, the chemical that promotes positive feelings of connection and empathy. Other neurological research indicates a happy ending causes the limbic part of the brain to release dopamine, the hormone that awakens feelings of optimism and hope. So make sure your past story focuses on their need and has a happy ending, thus satisfying them and leaving them feeling happy and relaxed.

So stories spark emotions chemically and psychologically. They stimulate our emotional side, the part that deals with intuition, as opposed to the rational part of our brain. It allows us to connect emotionally with our customers and build that rapport by engaging with that side of their character. Logic doesn't build rapport; emotion does and storytelling will greatly speed up that process.

Telling your customer a story also helps to put things into context and explain a maybe complex product, service or situation in a more meaningful light.

Stories work because they hark back to a more primitive time. They link us to the time of legends and myth, of fairy tales and heroes. As such they have a powerful effect on us at many levels and in many ways. Their power and effect should not be underestimated.

We are conditioned to think emotionally in metaphor and analogy. Stories bring that together in a frame of reference that is meaningful, understandable and engaging. This makes the message and connection stronger and more permanent than normal dialogue or conversation. Our storytelling taps into the imagination, developing our customer's shared experience with us, helping us build the rapport, provide clarity and bond with their needs and desires. Stories engage the listener in the narrative, offering a more powerful method of communication and understanding than a mere logical, left-brain discussion.

So, use your own vast knowledge and experience, or information and stories that you have heard from others. We have all had similar experiences, so with practice it is not difficult to naturally weave a relevant, honest, congruent, story into you conversation.

Using phrases that genuinely link your experience to that of the customer, telling a story will allow a relaxed, natural flow. Phrases such as 'That reminds me of…', 'I remember when…'. Or 'Imagine, if you will, a situation when I was…'. Before the punchline remember to ask the customer if they can imagine what happened next rather than telling them. This will engage their imagination and allow you to enhance your experience and theirs as well as enhance your fun and enjoyment.

Storytelling is a natural, powerful tool to help you continue to build rapport and allow that natural conversation to proceed to the complete exchange in either of the two ways we have already identified.

This then, is the end of our time at this station "Exchange" on our physical journey. We have continued to build rapport and had our natural conversation; and using S.M.I.L.E, N.I.C.E. C.H.A.T and PA.T.H., moved the customer through open questions, positive dialogue, while painting a picture and telling stories to a complete exchange.

The "desirous buying customer" will now join us at the next station "Transaction" where we will complete a revenue-enhancing conclusion; while the "Happy but unbuying customer" will be waiting for us at our last station "Nurture" further down the line, which we will come to soon.

We do need, however, to spend a few moments in the digital rather than physical environment and see what limitations and adaptations of the tools and model are required in this less favourable situation. Again, the aim is a complete exchange, as above in either of the two modes.

Digital and social media environment

The telephone call

Let us first consider the telephone call. We have built the initial rapport on the phone and are now developing that to complete an exchange. As before, we have now lost 55% of our communication, so we will have to focus more and work harder to ensure we complete our exchange. As such, we must use the tools we looked at in the "Rapport" station. **Active Listening Response Technique** is crucial to ensure we pick up every auditory clue from our customer to help us move our natural conversation along. We must also ensure we are in a place that is distraction free so we can focus all our attention on the call and gain the most from it. Please refer back to the previous chapter on how to do this.

Remember to smile while you are talking. One new tip: if you need to increase the energy and power of your conversation on the phone, either because of the product or service you offer, or to generate more energy for yourself (maybe it's been a long day), standing up, while talking can be a powerful tool. It will change the timbre of your voice by opening up the diaphragm; and standing up will make you feel less sluggish and more physically alert. All of this will be reflected in your voice and help create a stronger more positive energy down the phone, which the customer will pick up on. Regardless of whether you have used this before or not, do try it. You will be surprised at the difference.

Use the tools as above, to progress the natural conversation, the S.M.I.L.E., the N.I.C.E. C.H.A.T. and staying on the PA.T.H. to bring you to one of the two complete exchanges. You can still paint the picture using VAK on the phone, discuss value and tell a story. All of this is possible, with focus, congruence and control – our FCO^2 Formula. Though it is harder, the call can still take you to a complete exchange if you use the tools and follow the model.

So too with Skype

Skype has, as we stated, many advantages; it is free[with exceptions as mentioned before], you can speak to many people at the same time and share documents and desktops. It is as close to a face-to-face as you can come without actually being in the room. As such, because you are dealing with virtually the entire communications model, the rules of physical meeting (which we looked at above) apply.

As before, one caveat: you are not in the room with someone and as such the emotional content is not there in the same way. Even though they can see and hear you, they can't touch, smell or feel you. This means you need to focus even more on what you do see and what you hear, making up for that shortfall. So apply a mixture of the techniques from the physical to the **A**ctive **L**ist**e**ning **R**esponse **T**echnique, where they fit, and you will be able to build a positive response and have a more natural conversation.

As on the phone and in person, smiling and eye contact are very important here. Genuine smiles and strong, positive eye contact will enhance the feeling of interest, trust and rapport. Make sure your background is neutral and you don't have distractions such as noise, movement or unintended interruptions. You need to radiate even more positive energy to compensate for your customer not actually feeling, touching or smelling you. That said, Skype can be the means to complete the exchange using the tools just as we have in the physical arena.

Social media

Twitter cannot create an exchange as each communication is only 140 characters and any tweets should be steered as quickly as possible to other social media channels, a call or meeting.

LinkedIn is a useful professional environment, but I would try and move on to another platform to complete the exchange, as it is too impersonal for this part of the journey.

Facebook is the easiest, most relaxed and personal way to complete the exchange, if you have no other way of upgrading the contact to a call, Skype, or face-to-face meeting. As we mentioned before, mirror the level of formality, language and visuals to make the customer feel relaxed, safe and interested. Even with the advantages over other social media still see, if possible, whether you can convert the chat into a call, Skype or face-to-face maybe via your website or directly.

As we said previously, use the G.R.O.W.T.H.S. U.P. model and the tools and skills it offers, such as telling a story, painting a picture, smiling, respecting the individual and focusing on them to make sure that your message is attractive, relaxed, unique, captures the imagination and moves the natural conversation on to a complete exchange.

Finally we come to email. As before, as it is difficult to work with only 7% of the message, which means you are unlikely to build rapport on this platform. Exchange is only likely to happen if the customer wants something specific and is happy to conclude the transaction without any emotional input. In this case, you will move rapidly through this station and on to the next one down the track – "Transaction". Emails are not worthwhile communication platforms for building an emotional connection. Where possible they should only be used as an introduction, reminder or to provide written notification of a delivered product or service. Otherwise, and where possible, move the email onto a call, Skype or face-to-face for maximum results.

So, there we have it. In both the physical and digital world we have built on our stations of "Connect and Rapport" and completed our "Exchange". Now it is time to move on to the next station, "Transaction" where our "Desirous buying customer" – one of the two successful exchanges – will be waiting for us. We will leave the "Happy but unbuying customer" to wait at the "Nurture" station, where we will join them soon.

16 STATION 5 TRANSACTION

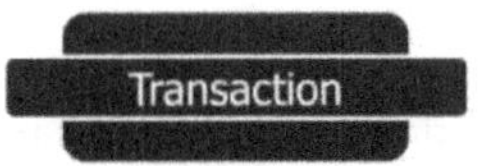

So, here we are; we have found our "undiscovered customer", connected with them as a "found customer", made that first contact, built rapport, made our exchange complete. One of those exchanges has led us to the "desirous buying customer", who by now is not just ready, but is also eager to complete this part of the journey by completing a transaction and becoming the "now complete customer". This station is about tying up the edges, securing the customer and generating increased revenue.

In the sales environment this is often the most stressful time, where you are forced to close, use scripts and aggressive techniques and then face the embarrassment, for some, of asking for the cash. All of this is because they are part of an unnatural process for many of you, where you feel no congruence and little control, leaving you, win or lose, feeling drained, embarrassed and drained of energy.

In contrast, in the G.R.O.W.T.H.S. U.P. model we have been following, and by using our simple tools, the transaction station is a naturally wanted result. It's a result of that safe environment, and the congruent, relaxed, focused approach that has lead this customer easily, safely, and with interest and respect, to exactly where they want to be. They have not been pushed or manipulated but supported, guided and helped so they feel eager to transact, are relaxed about the purchase and are happy with you and the product or service. Now that's a Win-Win.

You have understood the customer's need using our previous tools. As before, we will complete the transaction in the physical environment first before turning to the digital space.

Physical space

The transaction is a part of the conversation both of you want and is congruent for both of you. Completing the transaction flows naturally, not as a forced desperate attempt. Not to ask for this closure at this stage would leave you and the customer feeling incomplete and wanting. In this safe, anticipatory, mutually acceptable place – where details of the product or service needed are confirmed along with payment and delivery – rather than being embarrassing and awkward, it is the reverse. It is natural and flowing as both of you are congruent, happy to proceed and in a safe and secure place so to do.

Using our tool of C.H.A.T. and its open questions, you have now established the "Ws" so you know the following:

THE "6" W'S AND HOW -
OPEN QUESTIONS IN OUR NATURAL CONVERSATION.

All you need to do here is confirm the previous information so you know you have the right product or service at an agreed price as discussed in exchange. Ascertain how they wish to pay for it if you have options, i.e., cash, credit card, bank transfer, Paypal or whichever means applies. There should be no embarrassment or awkwardness here because the exchange has been agreed and it is at the stage where, if not previously obvious, the price should have been mentioned and confirmed as acceptable.

We are applying here our tool of C.H.A.T., both in asking "How" to complete the purchase and also in focusing on the last letter of C.H.A.T.

The last letter in C.H.A.T. flows naturally from the previous ones. We have clarified need, highlighted value and agreed an exchange. Now we are going to use **the "T" to Tie up the transaction**.

We have established previously that by clarifying the need and highlighting the value, if this value resonates with the customer as the "desirous buying customer", they will want an exchange, just as you do, that involves a purchase. In this case, we now have to ensure that exchange is brought to a natural and final conclusion by tying up the transaction. That is the exchange of value between two parties in business where mutual value is established and a need identified. This is satisfied by your product or service being transferred to the customer and your value being satisfied by the customer paying for that service or product.

There are of course some basic guidelines to ensure the transaction takes place. As you have not forced the customer to this point by pressure, scripts or manipulative techniques, the customer is ready to engage in a transaction willingly and even joyfully.

'**People love to buy but hate being sold to**.' This is exactly the situation your N.I.C.E. C.H.A.T., your natural conversation, has brought them to. So instead of the classic salesperson who dreads the close because of the pressure and atmosphere they have created, you, using the G.R.O.W.T.H.S. U.P. model, can ask for the transaction because your customer willingly and happily wants to buy. Indeed they may ask for the transaction to take place before you even get to mention it, as this is the natural consequence of your N.I.C.E. C.HA.T.

Consider this. It is essential that you both gain satisfaction by a clear conclusion because both of you want no loose ends and both of you want the transaction tied up. If the clarity of the transaction is not there then the customer will leave frustrated and you will feel disappointed. Your customer wants you to conclude the transaction. So ensure that you tie up any paperwork and where relevant obtain a signature and confirm payment and commitment. Your customer needs you to do this at this stage as they have happily agreed to the transaction and feel emotionally that they need completion. This is something to celebrate, unlike in old sales techniques where asking for the money or signature is often feared or avoided.

Once this is done, and as a natural conclusion to your chat, one which both of you want, then you can both feel warm and satisfied knowing your natural flow, your **N.I.C.E. C.H.A.T.** has taken both of you on a safe **PA.T.H.** to a great place where both of you wanted to be; feeling good, feeling the benefit.

You have a satisfied customer, not just for now but also for the future. You feel satisfied, relaxed and so good. So good that all you want is to do it again. What a contrast to those poor, aggressive, tired and drained salespeople.

Once you have asked for the money, completed the purchase, but do not make the mistake most anxious sales people do. Do not rush or try to get rid of the customer quickly. In sales processes, where there is manipulation and fear, there is a fear in the salesperson that if they stay with the customer after they have the money, the customer might smell a rat and realise they have been duped; so they get rid of them as fast as they can.

You are the opposite. The transaction has been a natural, enjoyable part of your conversation and a nice chat. Both of you feel happy, relaxed and energised by the completion of the transaction. Now is the time to spend time with the customer, making them feel even more special, lavishing the most rare of elements in business upon them – time and focus **after** you have completed the deal. This will cement your relationship, enhance both your feelings of wellbeing and take you and the customer, naturally, on to the final station on our journey, that of "Nurture".

Our station "Transaction", is a natural and welcomed outcome of a safe, relaxed environment that the G.R.O.W.T.H.S. U.P. model and its tools have provided, and which leaves both you and the customer relaxed, positive, energised and happy. What a contrast to old-style sales techniques, wouldn't you say?

Now let us conclude this station with the digital space.

The digital ad social media environment

Most of the rules, as indicated above and in previous stations, apply similarly here, so in brief:

The telephone call

Remember, you are still working with only 45% of our communication, so focus more and work harder to ensure the transaction is completed. Continue to use **Active Listening Response Technique**. Remember to still smile while you are talking. Use the tools as outlined above, to progress the natural conversation, the S.M.I.L.E., N.I.CE. C.H.A.T., and staying on the PA.T.H., to bring you to a complete transaction. Just as in the physical space, the customer has been naturally led here and wants to conclude the transaction as much as you do. Take time, lead the customer gently and ensure that you have clarified all of the details as to product, service, value and price. Ascertain how they wish to pay and have the item or service delivered. Once that is complete, and exactly as in the physical space, do not rush the last part of the exchange. Spend time talking to them, thanking them and relaxing with them – making both of you feel the conclusion was right, congruent and good. That way, even on the phone, you can move your customer on to the next station, "Nurture", as we shall see in the next chapter.

So too with Skype

Skype, as we stated before, has many advantages as it is as close to a face-to-face as you can come without actually being in the room. As such, because you are dealing with virtually all the communications model, the rules of physical meeting, looked at above, apply.

As before, one caveat: you are not in the room with someone and as such the emotional content is not there in the same way. Even though they can see and hear you, they can't touch, smell or feel you. This means you need to focus even more on what you do, see and what you hear, thus making up for that shortfall. So apply a mixture of the techniques from the physical to the **A**ctive **L**ist**e**ning **R**esponse **T**echnique, where they fit, and you will be able to build a positive response and have a more natural conversation.

As on the phone and in person, smiling and eye contact are very important here. Genuine smiles and strong, positive eye contact will enhance the feeling of interest, trust and rapport. Make sure your background is neutral and that you don't have distractions such as noise, movement or unintended interruptions. You need to radiate even more positive energy to compensate for your customer not actually feeling, touching or smelling you. That said, Skype can be the means to complete the transaction and move the customer on to the next station, using the tools, just as we have in the physical arena.

Social media

As we have stated, you cannot complete an exchange or transaction on Twitter as each communication is made up of only 140 characters. Thus responses to any tweets should be steered as quickly as possible to other social media, a call or meeting.

LinkedIn is, as we know, a professional environment. If you cannot move to another platform, completing the transaction here may be easier as it is a professional space where both parties are even more conditioned to expect that conclusion. Again, make your messaging clear and positive and do not rush once complete, but as above, build a connection as much as is possible for the next station along the line.

Facebook, as the most relaxed and personal platform is also easiest through which to complete the transaction – if you have no other way of upgrading the contact to a call, Skype session, or face-to-face meeting. Just as before, mirror the level of formality, language and visuals to make the customer feel relaxed, safe and interested. Focus on concluding the transaction by making sure you have complete clarity as to the product or service they want, the price charged and the delivery confirmation. Avoid ambiguity at this stage, as it will lead to a dissatisfied customer. If you can confirm with a call, Skype or face-to-face, do so.

Finally we come to email. Though it is difficult to work with only 7% of the message, and you are unlikely to build rapport on this platform, completing the transaction, as it is about detail of price, product, service, delivery and so on, may be possible, though it is not recommended here. At least both sides will have clarity, so ensure you are clear and concise and still try to see if you can follow up on another platform such as indicated above.

There it is. In both the physical and digital world we have used the G.R.O.W.T.H.S. U.P. model and applied its tools on our journey to our stations of "Connect and Rapport" and "Exchange". We have completed our transaction with the "Desirous buying customer", and feel energised, relaxed and positive, having generated more revenue and more customers. Now it is time to journey to our final station, "Nurture", where we will meet our "Happy unbuying customer" and take both them and the "Now complete customer" into our orbit by nurturing them for the future.

17 STATION 6 NURTURE

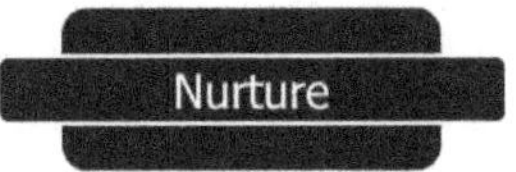

NURTURE

'Nurture the seed, nurture the need'

We have now reached the final station on our journey, though this is not the final location on our and our customer's journey. For it is here we build for the future. Using the model and relevant parts of the tools, we use this station to invest in each of our two customers. Whether they are the "Now complete" or "Happy but unbuying customer", it is here we treat both with equal respect and give each our precious commodity of time.

The big mistake in traditional sales techniques, as we have stated, is the over emphasis on "closing the sale" and not on nurturing a long-term relationship. G.R.O.W.T.H.S. U.P.is based on the premise that out natural conversation will lead via our journey of DisCRETioN to a situation where both customers, happy, relaxed and satisfied in their own way, wish to continue their relationship with us.

As an analogy, see yourselves as farmers not hunters. You are there to grow and nurture the seed of interest and nurture the need for satisfaction, not hunt down and kill your prey. Short termism, which is the basis for many sales scenarios, is pointless and self-defeating for us. Building your customer base for the future, just as you naturally build your business, is the focused, congruent and controlled way forward. This will lead to increased revenue and grow more customers.

So again, starting with the physical space, what do we need to say and do to nurture both our customers and maximise our future relationship with them? First we will look at some general methods for both and then some more specific for each before turning to how we will use the digital and social media space to continue that nurturing process.

We have completed the journey for both customers and now is the moment to spend time, not rush, however busy you may be. Customers remember the end of the process far more than the beginning, like some of us recall a film, play or concert, so make sure your last impression is as good as your first.

Imagine you have had an excellent meal in a good restaurant. You feel relaxed and sated and enjoying your post-dinner coffee when the head waiter comes over and tells you, without previous warning, that the table is booked and you have to leave – sorry. How would you feel? How would that affect the feelings you just had?

So ensure the customer leaves feeling happy, relaxed, safe, secure and feeling valued. That feeling of value for both customers will be as a result of the time and attention you have spent on them after the process of exchange and/or transaction has taken place.

So offer a coffee or tea where appropriate; make small talk and enquire as to future plans, shopping, holidays, anything relevant to the venue, product or service and previous discussion. Ensure they are feeling comfortable, energised and positive yet relaxed. After some general chat it is easy to ask for the following as part of our natural conversation:

Referrals

The absolutely best way to grow your business without stress or hassle is to be referred by an existing client to a potential new one. The beauty of referral is that you already have the innate credibility of the customer referring you. This means the N.O.I.S.E. you may encounter in your natural conversation will be greatly reduced, trust established quicker and more easily, and the whole journey of DisCRETioN will be simpler and even more effort free. You would think it was so obvious, yet why doesn't everyone do it?

I have come across seasoned salespeople who forget or are scared to ask for referrals. That is because they feel guilty about the sale or feel uncomfortable with their performance and the connection they have made.

Using our G.R.O.W.T.H.S. U.P. model, your natural conversation has created a safe, secure, relaxed atmosphere where the customer and you have built a relationship and it feels positive and relaxed. In this environment it is easy to ask for, and easy for them to give you, referrals.

I would say that every customer you talk to must be able to give you at least two to three people that they could refer you to, minimum. Just work out if every customer gives you that, how fast you can grow your revenue and business without extra effort. As an example: it may take you say, 100 phone calls to get 10 customer visits to get one purchase. In this example, one out of two referrals could easily gain you a complete customer, which requires much less effort and provides a better, easier result.

NURTURING RESULTS-REFERRALS A MINIMUM SUCCESS.
IF EACH CUSTOMER ONLY REFERS 2 IT
EASILY MULTIPLIES TO 4 AND MORE

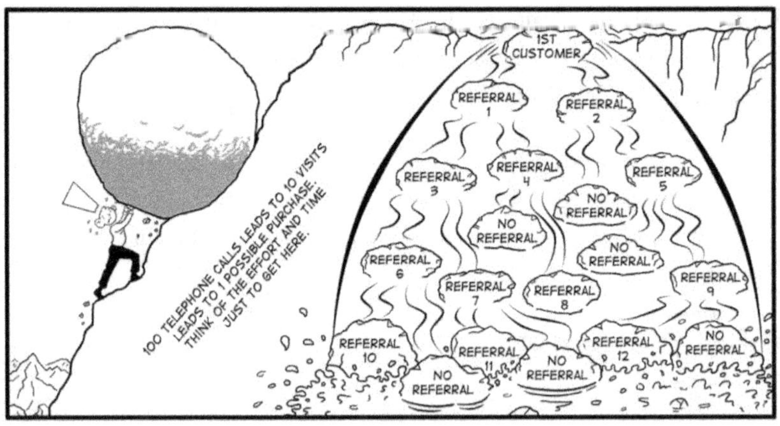

So, ask for the referral in a positive, relaxed way. For example, 'As you are happy with our services, or with what you have heard, do you know two or three people who might benefit from the same conversation?' Then make sure you get contact details, preferably a phone number and email. It's that simple. Thank them and move the conversation on; no pressure, just a natural end to a natural conversation. Easy.

Recommendations

Not so good as referrals but not to be sniffed at, this is where you don't ask for specific people to offer your services to, but enquire if the customer would be so kind as to recommend your service or product to someone they know. You can make this more attractive, if you wish, by telling them, that everyone that buys your product or service and mentions their name or gives you a card you give to them, entitles the existing customer to a free gift or discount next time. It costs you nothing, as they have to buy and so does you customer, but it feels like a reward for their help to you. A Win-Win.

Contact details

Whatever you do or say and whatever you do or don't ask for, make sure that every customer you speak to gives you their contact details including email, phone and business card, if relevant. This is the minimum you need to nurture them and grow your business easily. Customers who are happy and relaxed will feel no reluctance in giving you those details. How we use them we see below.

On this point, if you have a Twitter feed, LinkedIn or Facebook page or a website, while the customer is in front of you, help them sign up to or be given details of these resources because you want them to stay in touch, as we will see below. Don't forget, if it's Twitter they can sign up there and then on their mobile phone just as they can on Facebook, your website and other social media. Don't push it, but if the customer is happy with social media then they will be more than prepared to take advantage of it. If they are not just point out the advantage of keeping up to date with new offers and services. The best time to ensure they keep in touch is to sign them up when they are in front of you. Once they leave, their busy lives will interfere and they may forget. So seize the moment.

Invite back to event or sale

Finally, if you are holding a sale or special event, for existing customers, say, or a show of some kind, or are attending an exhibition, conference or event, make sure you let your customer know about it and where relevant give them a ticket to it or send them an invitation. This shows you value them and wish to continue the relationship. It will also get the customer back to you and let them see you, possibly in a different light; maybe giving a speech or being in a different environment where you show off your goods or services.

So, before the customer leaves and after you have completed the exchange and/or transaction, spend time to cultivate and nurture them so you extract the maximum benefit beyond the purchase; and leave them with a good feeling as they go about their business.

Before we get on to how to extend this nurturing into the digital space, a few words on the specific customers.

The now complete customer

This is the easy part now we have completed the transaction. They have received excellent value and feel good about themselves and their purchase. You are both in the optimum state of relaxed, positive, safe, energy to ask for the extras above and for you to nurture the client before they leave. Don't forget to thank them for their custom and ensure they do not need assistance when they leave to find a taxi or to carry the purchase to the car. If it is raining, do they have an umbrella? It's these little touches that stay with customers and build the future, for you and for them.

The happy but unbuying now customer

Here too, we have completed a worthwhile exchange; and even though the customer has not purchased anything, they are in a relaxed, positive mood, having been treated respectfully and as an individual. They understand your product or service and feel good about you and the time they have spent with you. As above, thank them for their time and ensure they have everything they need to go on with their day. The more courtesy and time you show to this customer, who has not made a purchase, the more likely they are to refer and recommend you – and come back when they do need what you offer. Time spent here is always worthwhile, so don't rush and stay positive.

That is the physical space, now we need to review the digital and social media space and how to use it to further nurture your customer,

The physical customer in the digital space

Let us here examine how to use the digital space to continue the nurturing of the physical customer and then turn to how we nurture the solely digital customer.

Regarding the physical customer: they have spent time with us and leave us feeling happy, relaxed and fulfilled. That is not the end of their story. However much information you received from them face-to-face, whether they purchased or not, it is now necessary to build on the bond you have created and keep the customer aware of you and your new or existing products or services. How do we do this?

Well hopefully, as discussed above, you have signed them up to all the relevant social media platforms you feature in. If you have done this then keeping in touch will be easy. If all you now have is their email address, then you need to proactively contact them, no more than one week after you last spoke to them. Use the email to thank them for visiting you and include in it any social media contact details you might have. Direct them to your website or Twitter feed.

Reassure them that as an existing or potential customer, registering on these sites will secure them better deals and access to more information to help them. Make it worth their while to sign up by offering a free gift or discount if they do so within a specified time period. Once they have signed up, make sure they are thanked and then receive regular but not intrusive messages in the relevant form to tell them what is happening. As an example, if you start a Facebook or LinkedIn group as a means of discussing information concerning your products or services, make sure you invite them to join and then make sure the group is kept up to date regularly with new ideas and information. If, for example, you are having a show, sale or event, this is the place you can highlight it and invite them to join you in the flesh. The digital reinforces the physical and vice versa.

If you have found them on social media, on Facebook, LinkedIn or Twitter, maybe consider contacting them and asking if you can follow them, if and only if appropriate: you don't want to be seen to stalk your customer, but you do want them to feel included and informed.

This all takes time but remember, 'nurture the seed, nurture the need' and your existing customers, who are often worth at least five potential ones, will stay with you longer, purchase more and recommend others. It is always time well spent.

Finally, a brief word on the digital customer and how to continue the digital contact through to "Nurture" and more. As in past stations, we have developed our digital journey within the limitations and with the advantages it has afforded us. However, that journey has progressed and at this last station we can 'nurture the seed, nurture the need' in many ways.

Phone call

If our journey has been on the phone, then make a follow-up call after a transaction or exchange, thank the person, see if there is anything else they need and if appropriate, ask for referrals or recommendations. We can also suggest that communication would be better if they came and saw our premises if possible; or if not, that they looked at us on social media. We could give them our details or ask them for their email address, so we could send them information and follow up as mentioned above.

The Skype customer

Again, in the last call they can be thanked and nurtured almost as in the physical environment, though without a cup of tea, of course. There is no reason why, in this positive, natural exchange, that we cannot ask for all the detail we have suggested in their physical world. See if you can sign them up to your social media platforms there and then during the call as they are on their computer, tablet or phone. Further follow-up will depend on what they do. The minimum should be a Skype text message and then, maybe, after an appropriate time, say a week, a call. The call is to see if circumstances have changed or if you can help in any way. If you can invite them to a physical meeting or event, then obviously that would be ideal.

LinkedIn or Facebook?

LinkedIn is harder to nurture but not impossible. Make sure you keep in touch, maybe get them to join a group you run on LinkedIn or join one of their groups, if relevant, to keep in touch with them and see what is happening in their world. Obviously, again try and convert this platform to a Skype call or face-to-face meeting if you can. Whatever you do, do not lose touch. Maybe keep them as a contact and message them every now and then, directing them to your website or other media when you have new products services or events. You are in it for the long haul and patience definitely applies here.

Facebook is more personal, is easier to message, like, share and post and is useful for directing contacts to your other social media platforms. Try and get them to sign up to them while in Facebook conversations and make sure that you keep them in the loop as to new offerings by linking them, where relevant, to the website, page or Twitter feed.

Twitter is difficult to use for nurturing but can be a good tool to continue to put out messages advising your customers about new ideas, events products or services. Encourage them to follow you and convert to another platform, maybe by offering discounts or gifts for sign-ups.

Finally email. This is excellent for keeping in touch and advising people of new offers and events. However, it should be supported by other social media platforms or converted into a physical event or meeting to reinforce the nurturing process. Email is good for information and reinforcing a message but cannot replace the personal touch. Again, be patient. Keep people in the loop without hassling them and play the long game.

So there it is, our journey of DisCRETioN has completed this cycle and you are ready to continue with the next customer. Our natural conversation, the G.R.O.W.T.H.S. U.P. model, has taken you to this final station with ease and congruence leaving you refreshed, energised and ready for more. In our final chapter we will review the tools, the journey and the model and ensure that your G.R.O.W.T.H.S. U.P. will and can happen.

Section 4 Conclusion

18 CONCLUSION AND HOW TO EXTEND THE MODEL

Well we have completed the first cycle of our journey using the model, learning about the tools and applying them on our journey. Our natural conversation that starts with a smile and ends with a nurtured customer is, as you can hopefully now see, an exciting, positive, yet relaxed and safe method for generating revenue and increasing customers without the hassle of sales whilst uplifting performance. G.R.O.W.T.H.S. U.P. works because if you understand it, internalise it, practice it and apply it, it allows that natural conversation to take you and your customer on a gentle, congruent journey that can only lead to a positive outcome whether or not they purchase.

Sales is never your goal or target so don't get fixated on that target or KPI; it will only set you up to fail. Your only target is having the natural conversation that will lead to one of our two exchanges. Just the N.I.C.E. C.H.A.T. is success. If your customer goes away feeling good about themselves as well as you and what you offer, then you have succeeded to grow your business and create opportunity for future revenue generation and customer growth.

Just keep having that natural conversation with anyone and everyone you encounter. Because it is an effortless activity to not be bound by desperate goals or unrealistic targets, because there is no failure, then it is easy to chat to more people and in more situations.

We have looked at how you connect with someone who enters your premises or whom you contact online. In this conclusion, before we review the model and its tools, I want to show you how you can extend that natural conversation and the model to give you an even greater chance to get more and more customers in more diverse situations.

You are obviously passionate about your product or service and can talk about it endlessly and with ease, I am sure. Now we are going to harness that knowledge and passion – and using our model – extend the natural conversation further away from the natural work place to the wider community.

For some of you this will be easier than for others. The more extrovert and comfortable you are being with others the simpler this will be. If you are naturally shy or introverted or find it harder to communicate with strangers then this might take a little work after which you will find it easy and even fun.

It's all about opportunity and our old friend from FCO^2 focus. Have you ever noticed that when you try to diet all the ads on TV are about food, or if you buy a new car you notice how many of that make or model seem to be on the road? We already stated the NLP saying that 'energy flows where attention goes.' This is about using that attention and energy to spot opportunity and have that natural conversation in places and situations you might not expect to be possible. The one other element you need to successfully extend the model into the wider arena is a PMA. Now we have already looked at the power of PMA in our chapter on that subject. Suffice it to say here, that when you are in a positive mood and the sun is shining, you are more likely to see an opportunity and exploit it than if you are in a negative mood and see the world as grey.

Darren Brown, the well-known illusionist, offered a great example of this in his Channel 4 programme *The Secret Of Luck* by illustration of an experiment Richard Wiseman mentions in his book *The Luck Factor*. He placed a note of money, I'm not sure if it was £5 or £10, on the pavement outside a restaurant. He had previously interviewed several people, some whom were labelled unlucky and some lucky. In most cases the lucky ones saw the note and used it effectively while the unlucky ones did not even notice it. The point, and if you want more information as to what makes lucky people, I recommend Richard Wisemans great book *The Luck Factor*. The point is that some people look for opportunity while others see life as lacking in opportunity and don't look for the chance or the potential.

So start looking for the money on the ground (metaphorically speaking) and the signs around you. Use your focus to look for opportunity with a positive attitude and expect it to occur. Remember, 'Energy flows where attention goes.' Be open to opportunity and it will be there waiting for you to take advantage of.

You are probably wondering what I am talking about in relation to opportunity and extending the natural conversation – unless you broke off to watch Darren Brown or read Wiseman's book.

Let me give you some examples of extending the opportunity and having the natural conversation in surprising places.

You run an employment agency and are looking for a new assistant for your client's coffee shop. You happen to be having a coffee in a coffee shop (not the client's), maybe doing business or talking to a friend. You are served by an excellent waiter or waitress. They are personable and efficient. You also hear some gossip among the staff they are not happy at this shop because, say, the owner treated them badly. If you are not looking for opportunity you will shrug, finish your coffee and leave. If you are tuned in, positive and looking for that opportunity, you will talk to the waiter or waitress, find out if they would be interested in another opportunity and get them an interview. What a lucky chance you might say: it never happens. I promise you it does and more than you realise, if you sensitise yourself to the possibility.

I used to hire salespeople. Where did I find my best recruits? In hotels among underpaid but enthusiastic waiting staff. Once I saw the opportunity, and didn't just treat the hotel as somewhere to stay and leave, I recruited some of my best people there.

Another example. You run a cosmetics shop. You have just got a new cream that is great for treating a variety of ailments (you decide what). You happen to be out on your lunch break or spending the weekend with friends. While you are chatting you hear someone, even at another table, or easier, one of your circle, mentioning they are having problems that you know this cream could help. If you are switched off – and not looking for opportunity – you will fail to really notice the comment and carry on enjoying yourself. If you are looking for the opportunity, you will lean over and just say something like, 'I couldn't help overhearing you and the problem you mentioned. I have just got in a fantastic cream that might help. Here are my details. If you would like to pop in, I will personally serve you and make sure you select the cream that's right for you.' This is not being pushy. Rather, it's just recognising an opportunity and offering to help in a natural, caring and positive way. You might get another customer and you know what, if you treat them according to the model, you might get a lot of referrals too. And all from seeing and hearing the opportunity and being sensitive to the infinite possibilities out there.

One more example: this combines your passion and your knowledge and is what a lot of network marketing or MLM [Multi Level Marketing] consultants do. Don't worry, it is not selling, just recognising the opportunity. If this feels like a step too far and you are uncomfortable with it then please feel free to not try it till you are even happier with the model.

You are on a train or bus, or waiting in a station or having a meal or coffee; and there is someone opposite or next to you and you say no more than 'good morning afternoon', etc. If they seem ready to talk then have a chat, a natural conversation, no more. If they don't respond, then go on back to reading your book, Kindle or tablet. If they are happy to chat, and many people are (more than you would think), ask the natural question after a while which is, 'what do you do or where are you from?'

If they do something that means they might benefit from your product or service then why not just say, 'oh, that's interesting. I make widgets or sell ice cream or offer tax advice.' Nothing more; a natural conversation like you would have with a friend, colleague or anyone. You will be amazed at how many people then say, 'oh, I really need a good widget or ice cream or I've got real tax problems.' All you said was good morning and that allowed the natural conversation to go where it wanted; not forced in any way, just a smooth flow.

The point is to expect and to react proactively to an opportunity if it presents itself – as opposed to ignoring it or not saying good morning because of the mindset that makes you think that this kind of luck never happens to me. Use the model, have that natural conversation and where appropriate, use your passion for your product and your knowledge will convert opportunity into a potential customer. You never know. But for sure, as they say in the UK National Lottery: 'You have to be in it to win it.' Be sensitive and open to opportunity and you will be luckier than you realise. So extend the model and your natural conversation outward to any situation where an opportunity may be waiting, even though you don't realise it. And always carry your business card, even on holiday; you will be amazed who you bump into.

So, we have now used the model in premises and in the physical space, in social media, digital and telephone environments. We just need to recap the tools and the journey to ensure you are completely clear how to learn, internalise, and use the G.R.O.W.T.H.S. U.P. model. This will ensure you do generate more revenue and greater customer numbers.

This book has been about introducing you to the G.R.O.W.T.H.S. U.P. model. We started by understanding that G.R.O.W.T.H.S. U.P. stands for: Generating Revenue Without The Hassle of Sales whilst Uplifting Performance. We explained that the model replaces old-style aggressive, combative sales processes and sales targets based on revenue and replaces it with a natural method to increase the number of your customers and improve your revenue generation while staying relaxed, focused, congruent and motivated. The book outlined what G.R.O.W.T.H.S. U.P. was as an overview of the model, introducing you to some of the underlying concepts and trends. It then highlighted some reasons why you might hate sales and how the model replaces those hates with something positive and substantive: concepts that motivate and reinforce your well-being and boost your self-image.

After that we identified and discarded some bad habits, old thoughts and old-style thinking, to clear the way to help you gain the most traction from the G.R.O.W.T.H.S. U.P. model. To reinforce that clarity, in Section 2, we began by helping you have a PMA – Positive Mental Attitude; essential to help you maximise the model. We offered tips and techniques to get you feeling positive. We showed you ways to stay there, by reinforcing your self-image, improving your motivation helping you stay focused, congruent and in control.

The rest of that section offered you a series of techniques to obtain the best results. Using easy to remember acronyms, we learnt how to S.M.I.L.E. and then how to have that natural conversation by having a N.I.C.E. C.H.A.T. We explored the concept of N.O.I.S.E. and how, by understanding and breaking through it, you can stay relaxed, positive and help generate more revenue and customers.

We added to this, by learning how staying on the right PA.T.H. helps with your conversations, exchanges and transactions. Finally, in that section, we brought it all together by introducing you to the FCO² Formula of Focus, Congruence and Control, which combined with the G.R.O.W.T.H.S. U.P. model brings you maximum return while staying energised, happy and productive.

In Section 3, we applied the G.R.O.W.T.H.S. U.P. model by taking you on a journey of DisCRETioN, where at each station we demonstrated how to apply the tools to naturally generate more customers and revenue. We explored both the physical and digital space and their advantages and limitations, in maximising your revenue generation and your natural conversation.

This section, our conclusion, is where we have brought all of what we have discovered together and learnt how to extend that natural conversation and the model into the larger and often overlooked, wider space.

Section 5 is a resource; a series of appendices that will include the full list of acronyms; some visual models referred to in the book; exercises to help you stay positive, remove stress, help you sleep better, stay focused, congruent and in control.

Finally, thank you for purchasing and reading this book, whether on Kindle or hard copy. I hope it will give you a stress-free future where your G.R.O.W.T.H.S. U.P. If you have any questions or comments, would like further advice or support, or to sign up to one of my workshops or coaching opportunities, please email me at growthsup@gmail.com or visit my website and contact me there: www.growthsup.co.uk. Tweet me: @copewellbeing or follow me on Facebook at: www.facebook.com/copewellbeingsgrowthsup. You will also find updates and video blog tips there to help enhance your reading experience.

Appendices

Appendix i – Noise Models

i) How we filter information from the NLP model of distort, delete, generalise.

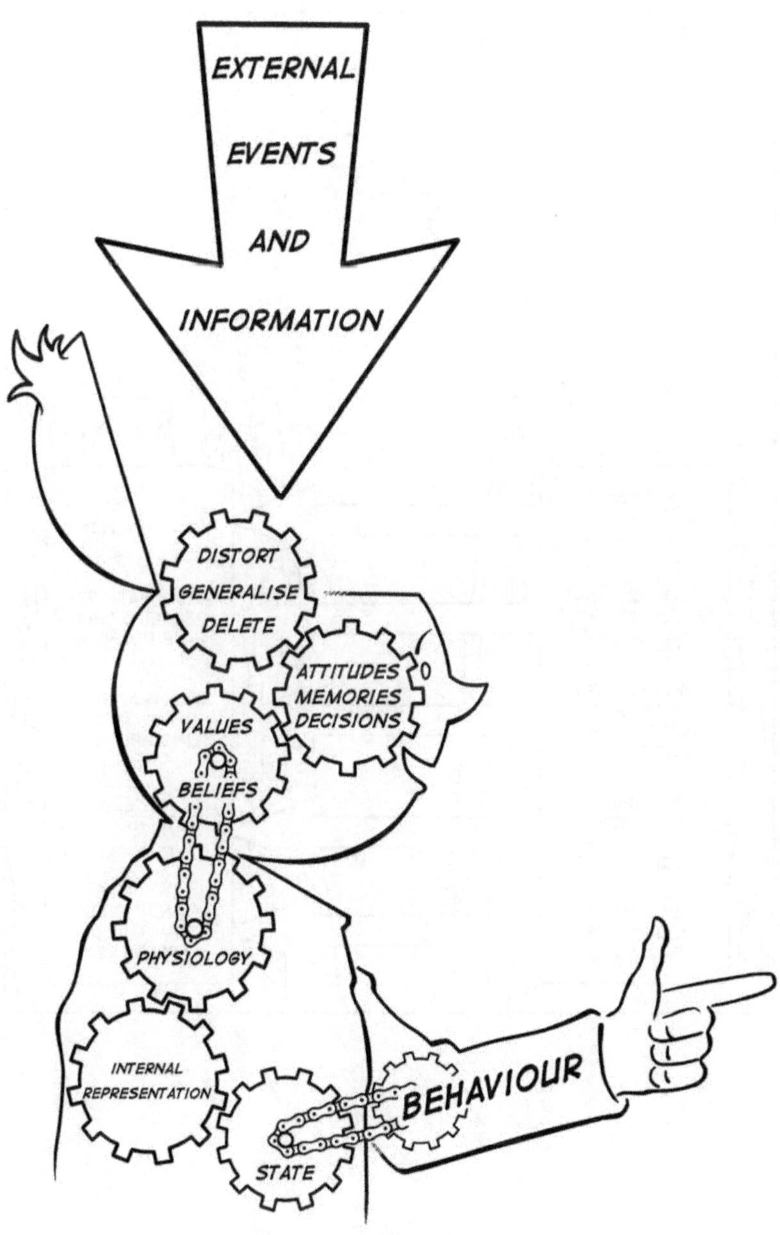

Avoiding gaps in perception between what we say and what people hear.

AVOIDING PERCEPTION GAPS

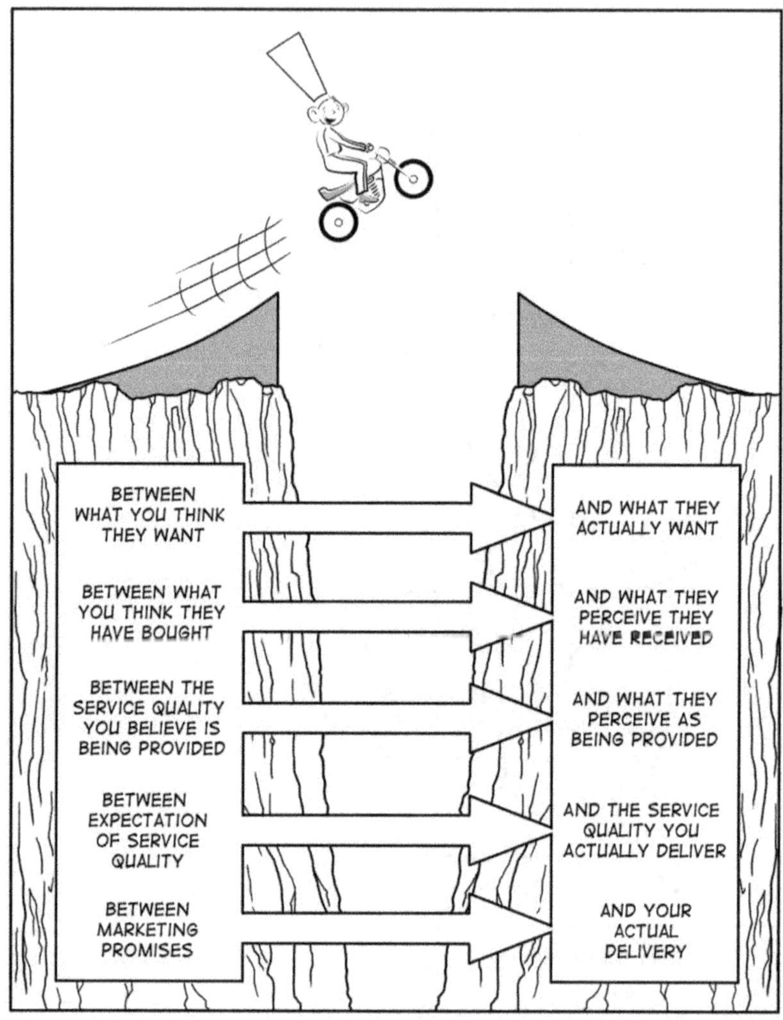

How Noise distorts communication.

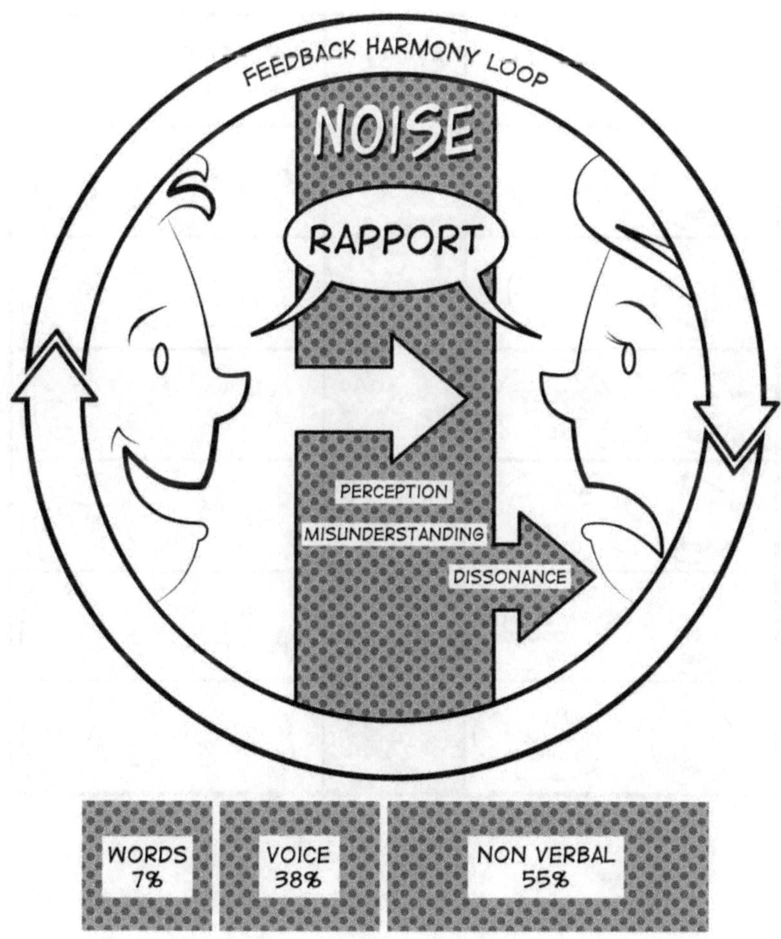

NOISE DISTORTION OF WHAT YOU SAY AND WHAT YOUR CUSTOMER HEARS IF IN A NEGATIVE STATE ETC.

WHAT YOU SAY	*NOISE* PERCEPTION MISUNDERSTANDING	*WHAT THEY HEAR IF IN A NEGATIVE STATE OR HAVE OBSTINATE BELIEFS ETC*
GOOD MORNING		WHAT'S GOOD ABOUT IT ?
A LOVELY DAY		NOT FOR ME
WHICH COLOUR DO YOU MOST LIKE ?		WHAT'S IT TO YOU ?
WE HAVE THAT ON SPECIAL OFFER		OH A RIP OFF PRICE
WHAT ELSE MIGHT YOU BE LOOKING FOR ?		TRYING TO SELL MORE OF WHAT I DON'T WANT
WHEN WOULD YOU LIKE IT DELIVERED ?		WHY ARE YOU PUSHING ME ?

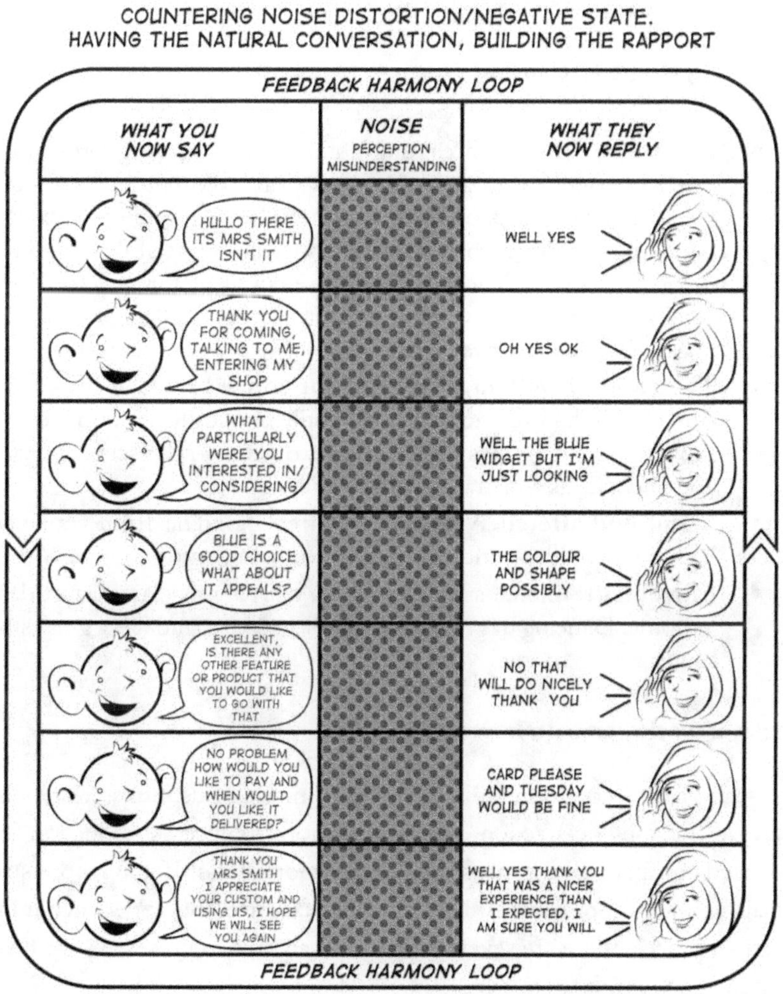

COUNTERING NOISE DISTORTION/NEGATIVE STATE.
HAVING THE NATURAL CONVERSATION, BUILDING THE RAPPORT

FEEDBACK HARMONY LOOP

WHAT YOU NOW SAY	NOISE PERCEPTION MISUNDERSTANDING	WHAT THEY NOW REPLY
HULLO THERE ITS MRS SMITH ISN'T IT		WELL YES
THANK YOU FOR COMING, TALKING TO ME, ENTERING MY SHOP		OH YES OK
WHAT PARTICULARLY WERE YOU INTERESTED IN/ CONSIDERING		WELL THE BLUE WIDGET BUT I'M JUST LOOKING
BLUE IS A GOOD CHOICE WHAT ABOUT IT APPEALS?		THE COLOUR AND SHAPE POSSIBLY
EXCELLENT, IS THERE ANY OTHER FEATURE OR PRODUCT THAT YOU WOULD LIKE TO GO WITH THAT		NO THAT WILL DO NICELY THANK YOU
NO PROBLEM HOW WOULD YOU LIKE TO PAY AND WHEN WOULD YOU LIKE IT DELIVERED?		CARD PLEASE AND TUESDAY WOULD BE FINE
THANK YOU MRS SMITH I APPRECIATE YOUR CUSTOM AND USING US, I HOPE WE WILL SEE YOU AGAIN		WELL YES THANK YOU THAT WAS A NICER EXPERIENCE THAN I EXPECTED, I AM SURE YOU WILL

FEEDBACK HARMONY LOOP

Appendix ii – Stress Triggers and Tips

Stress relieving exercises

- **Breathing.** Though breathing comes naturally, deep breathing is often overlooked as an exercise; it's an excellent stress reducer. Breathe in while tucking in your tummy and feel the air as it expands your lungs and your chest. Breathe in to the count of three and hold it for two counts. Then exhale to the count of three. Take two to three deep breathes several times a day and soon daily stress triggers may well be blown away.
- **Take a brief walk in your lunch or coffee break.** A brisk ten or fifteen minute walk each day is not only physically good for you, but moves your focus away from your problems to the scenery around you and aids as a distraction and stimulant.
- **Stand and stretch.** Visualize the stress flooding from your back, legs and shoulders, and pour out of your fingertips and toes.
- **Movement.** Join an aerobics class, a martial arts class or just dance at home. Dancing has two advantages: exercise, and it is a great stress reducer.

Stress at work – tips on how to control it

Stress at work is common and damaging to many of us. Stress results in a decrease in job satisfaction and motivation, reduced production and increased conflicts, which inevitably lead to more stress! If you ignore stress signals you are more liable to become ill or fatigued and experience injury. As an employee, there are several steps you can take to preserve your health by reducing workplace stress.

External triggers

Stress can be caused by something that seems as small as an incorrectly positioned chair or computer screen. Other examples of external triggers include loud or continuous noise, overheated or cold conditions, nosy or noisy co-workers, demanding bosses, and complaining customers. If external triggers are causing problems for you, the worst thing you can do is ignore them. Identify and examine external triggers for possible solutions. Even if all of them aren't resolved, any positive change you make will result in a happier, healthier you.

Internal triggers

Internal triggers can be feelings of irritability, dissatisfaction, inability, or the feeling that your efforts aren't properly rewarded or recognized. One helpful way to reduce internal stress is to remember what you liked about your job when you started it. Consider what has changed as well as what needs to change for you to be satisfied again.

Other tips to avoid stress at work

1. Condition yourself to wake and get ready, not for your work, but for your day.
2. When driving to work, listen to music, comedy, self-help CDs – anything that isn't related to work.
3. Take an alternative route to your work. A change in scenery will help you stay alert and keep you focused.
4. Instead of coffee, drink water, juice or electrolyte-infused liquids. Dehydration is often the cause of fatigue. Coffee and soft drinks that contain caffeine may seem to "keep you going", but in reality they add to stress and don't keep your body hydrated.
5. As you plan your work, plan your time away from work. At the end of the day, leave work behind you and focus on your plans for the evening. Work to live. Relaxation away from work means less stress… and a better day tomorrow!

More tips to avoid stress – a relaxation routine

Planning your relaxation reduces anxiety and helps your body and mind recover from everyday stress. Long soaks in a bath, listening to music or a walk in the park do the trick for some. As an alternative, try a relaxation or meditation class.

22 Stress reducing tips that work

1. Get up fifteen minutes earlier in the morning. The inevitable morning mishaps will be less stressful.
2. Prepare for the morning the evening before. Set the breakfast table, make lunches, select and leave out the clothes you plan to wear.
3. Write down appointment times; don't rely on your memory about when to collect items or do chores.

4. Be prepared to wait. A paperback can make a wait in a post office line almost pleasant.
5. Procrastination is stressful. Whatever you want to do tomorrow, do today. Whatever you want to do today, do it now.
6. Allow extra time to get to appointments.
7. Eliminate (or restrict) the amount of caffeine in your diet.
8. Always set up contingency plans – "just in case."
9. Relax your standards. The world will not end if the house doesn't get completely cleaned this weekend.
10. Say 'No!'. Saying 'no' to extra activities or events you don't have time for reduces stress; everyone needs quiet time to relax and be alone.
11. Unplug your phone. Want to take a long bath, meditate, sleep, or read without interruption? Drum up the courage to temporarily disconnect. (The possibility of there being a terrible emergency in the next hour or so is almost zero.) Or use an answering machine.
12. Get enough sleep.
13. Talk about it. Discussing your problems can help clear your mind of confusion so you can concentrate on problem solving.
14. Learn to live one day at a time. Live in the Now.
15. Every day, do one thing you really enjoy.
16. Do something for somebody else.
17. Become more flexible.
18. Eliminate destructive self-talk and self-limiting statements.
19. Do one thing at a time. When you are with someone, be with that person and with no one or nothing else. When you are busy with a project, concentrate on doing that project and forget about everything else you have to do.
20. If an especially unpleasant task faces you, do it early in the day and get it over with. Then the rest of your day will be free of anxiety.
21. Learn to delegate responsibility to capable others. Have a forgiving view of events and people. Accept the fact that we live in an imperfect world.
22. Have an optimistic view of the world. Believe that most people are doing the best they can.

Appendix iii – Exercises

Here are some exercises to help you relax, sleep better and stay de-stressed. All of which is designed to help you stay focused, congruent, in control and in a positive frame of mind. They can be read or read into a recording devise and played back. They will also be on my video blogs, which you can listen to on my website: www.growthsup.co.uk.

Relaxation exercise

Let us first take a minute together to enjoy a moment of rest and relaxation.

As you listen to my voice, sit comfortably with your eyes closed if you wish and allow yourself a few minutes of total warm and complete relaxation. Let's just get our breathing relaxed too with this exercise, which you know so well by now:

Breathe in – hold for two seconds, think count of one – breathe out slowly and deeply.

Breathe in – hold for two seconds, think count of two – breathe out slowly and deeply.

Breathe in – hold for two seconds, think count of three – breathe out slowly and deeply and as you breathe out, think about how your body is relaxing.

Breathe in –hold for two seconds, think count of four – breathe out slowly and deeply – and feel how heavy your feet feel against the ground.

Breathe in – hold for two seconds, think count of five – breathe out slowly and deeply – and feel how heavy and relaxed your thighs feel against the chair.

Breathe in – hold for two seconds, think count of six – breathe out slowly and deeply – if your eyes feel heavy and you want to close them

DO SO NOW or whenever you wish.

Breathe in – hold for two seconds, think count of seven – breathe out slowly and deeply – and feel how heavy and relaxed your back and bottom feel against the chair – heavy and relaxed like your closed eyes.

Breathe in – hold for two seconds, think count of eight – breathe out slowly and deeply – and feel how heavy your arms and shoulders feel; heavy and totally relaxed with each breath.

Breathe in – hold for two seconds, think count of nine – breathe out slowly and deeply – and feel how your whole body is relaxed from your feet to your head; relaxed yet focused.

Breathe in – hold for two seconds, think count of 10 – breathe out slowly and deeply – and feel how your mind is clear and ready to learn, while your body stays totally relaxed.

Now just keep breathing slowly and deeply while your mind stays deeply focused on peaceful relaxation and your body continues to remain delightfully, wonderfully, relaxed.

When you are ready count backwards from 3 to 1 and open your eyes. Feel how relaxed and at peace you are. Stay still for 5 minutes enjoying that wonderful floating feeling. Then have a glass of water and resume your busy day.

Sleep exercise

Ok. So for this exercise you need to be lying on your bed, ready for sleep. Lie on your back, lights dim or off and with no distractions if possible such as the radio or TV, noisy neighbours, screaming kids – you get the idea. Are you ready, lying on your back, comfortable? Excellent. Then let's begin.

This is an exercise in relaxation of body and mind and by the end you will be able to fall naturally into a deep, relaxed sleep. As you are lying there first begin by getting your breathing slow and steady. You know how. Breathe in slowly and deeply, hold for two seconds and breathe out fully. Let's first repeat that ten times to get you full relaxed.

After that we will use the tensing and relaxing of your body to ensure you fall easily and naturally into a wonderful deep, satisfying sleep. If you feel yourself slipping into sleep at any time, let it happen. You do not need to complete the exercise.

So… breathe in – hold for two seconds, think count of one – breathe out slowly and deeply.

Breathe in – hold for two seconds, think count of two – breathe out slowly and deeply.

Breathe in – hold for two seconds, think count of three – breathe out slowly and deeply – and as you breathe out think about how your body is relaxing

Breathe in – hold for two seconds, think count of four – breathe out slowly and deeply – and feel how heavy your feet feel resting on the bed.

Breathe in – hold for two seconds, think count of five – breathe out slowly and deeply – and feel how heavy and relaxed your thighs feel against the bed.

Breathe in – hold for two seconds, think count of six – breathe out slowly and deeply – if your eyes feel heavy and you want to close them DO SO NOW or whenever you wish.

Breathe in – hold for two seconds, think count of seven – breathe out slowly and deeply – and feel how heavy and relaxed your back and bottom feel against the bed, heavy and relaxed like your closed eyes.

Breathe in – hold for two seconds, think count of eight – breathe out slowly and deeply – and feel how heavy your arms and shoulders feel; heavy and totally relaxed with each breath.

Breathe in – hold for two seconds, think count of nine – breathe out slowly and deeply – and feel how your whole body feels relaxed from your feet to your head; relaxed and at peace.

Breathe in – hold for two seconds, think count of 10 – breathe out slowly and deeply – and feel how your mind is quiet and ready for sleep, while your body stays deeply and totally relaxed.

Now just keep breathing slowly and deeply while your mind stays deeply quiet and your body continues to remain, delightfully, wonderfully, deeply, relaxed.

Wonderful. Now keeping your breathing relaxed and slow, and feel yourself drifting off into sleep.

Start with your toes and tense and relax your left toes twice. That's it, tense and relax, tense and relax.

Now your left foot: tense and relax, tense and relax.

Now move up to your left leg: tense and relax, tense and relax.

Now your left thigh: tense and relax, tense and relax. That's it, feel how wonderfully heavy and relaxed your body is and how peaceful and quiet your mind is all the while still focusing on just my voice and on tensing and relaxing – nothing else.

Now your chest: tense and relax tense and relax. That's it.

Now your left shoulder: tense and relax, tense and relax.

Now your left arm: tense and relax, tense and relax. Yes, and now your left hand: tense and relax, tense and relax. Excellent. Slowly drift to

sleep; your body wonderfully heavy, your eyes heavy and relaxed, your mind at peace as you clench and relax your eyelids; tense and relax as your eyes stay firmly, deeply shut…

And now for the right side of your body.

Start with your right toes and tense and relax them twice. That's it; tense and relax, tense and relax.

Now your right foot: tense and relax, tense and relax.

Now move up to your right leg: tense and relax, tense and relax.

Now your right thigh: tense and relax, tense and relax. That's it; feel how wonderfully heavy and relaxed your body is and how peaceful and quiet your mind is, all the while still focusing on just my voice and on tensing and relaxing – nothing else.

Now your chest: tense and relax, tense and relax. That's it.

Now your right shoulder: tense and relax, tense and relax.

Now your right arm: tense and relax, tense and relax.

Now your right hand: tense and relax, tense and relax. Excellent. Now slowly drift to sleep; your body wonderfully heavy, your eyes heavy and relaxed, your mind at peace as you clench and relax your eyelids; tense and relax as your eyes stay firmly, deeply shut…

As you fall into a deep, relaxed, warm and wonderful natural sleep, know that as you sleep through the night with your body and mind rested and at peace, you will awaken refreshed and energised, ready for a wonderful, new day.

Stress relief exercise

As you listen to my voice, sit, stand or lie comfortably and relaxed. Close your eyes if it's safe to do so and allow yourself a few minutes of Total warm and complete relaxation, free from any stress that might be near. Let's just get our breathing relaxed too with this exercise, which you know so well now:

Breathe in – hold for two seconds, think count of one – breathe out slowly and deeply.

Breathe in – hold for two seconds, think count of two – breathe out slowly and deeply.

Breathe in – hold for two seconds, think count of three – breathe out slowly and deeply – and as you breathe out think about how your body is relaxing.

Breathe in – hold for two seconds, think count of four – breathe out slowly and deeply – and feel how heavy your feet feel against the ground. Now see your body as a strong oak tree. Your body is solid like the wide, brown trunk of the tree. Imagine sturdy roots growing from your legs and going down deeply into the earth, anchoring your body. You feel solid and strong, able to handle any stress.

Breathe in – hold for two seconds, think count of five – breathe out slowly and deeply – and feel how heavy your thighs feel and how – relaxed and strong and anchored to the earth like a strong, wide, powerful, oak tree, you feel its strength.

Breathe in – hold for two seconds, think count of six – breathe out slowly and deeply. If your eyes feel heavy and you want to close them, DO SO NOW or whenever you wish, letting your energy flow through you; grounding you to the earth as an oak tree and its roots stay grounded to the earth.

Breathe in – hold for two seconds, think count of seven – breathe out slowly and deeply – and feel how heavy and relaxed the rest of your body feels with energy flowing from top to bottom, relaxed and calm, grounded in the earth as the oak tree – strong and powerful.

Breathe in – hold for two seconds, think count of eight –breathe out slowly and deeply – and feel how heavy your arms and shoulders feel; heavy and totally relaxed with each breath with energy flowing calmly through from your head to your toes; your feet in contact with the ground – grounded in the earth as the oak tree has its roots grounded in the soil.

Breathe in – hold for two seconds, think count of nine – breathe out slowly and deeply – and feel how your whole body is relaxed, from your feet to your head; relaxed yet focused

Breathe in – hold for two seconds, think count of 10 – breathe out slowly and deeply – and feel how your mind is clear and calm; free from tension or stress, your body and mind ready to continue, whatever the situation, grounded and calm, strong as the oak, grounded, aware; safe and secure as the oak tree, able to stay calm and relaxed whatever the situation.

Now just keep breathing slowly and deeply while your mind stays deeply calm and your body continues to remain delightfully, wonderfully, relaxed.

Wonderful. Now you are in the right frame to continue. Now you can open your eyes – enjoy the wonderful sensation of strength and calm, totally relaxed and able to deal with whatever situation presents itself.

Appendix iv – List of Acronyms and their Definitions

S.MI.L.E.

- S – Start with a smile
- M – Make eye contact
- I – Individualise
- L – Look, listen, lead
- E – Engage

N.I.C.E.

- N – Natural
- I – Individual
- C – Clarify alignment
- E – Exchange

C.H.A.T.

- C – Clarify need
- H – Highlight values
- A – Agree exchange
- T – Tie up transaction

N.O.I.S.E.

- N – Negative expectations
- O – Obstinate beliefs
- I – Individual image (self worth)
- S – Scared state
- E – Experiences in the past

Pa.T.H.

- Pa – Paint a picture
- T – Tell a story
- H – Have a conversation

FCO[2]

- Focus
- Congruence
- Control

DisCRETioN

Discover, Connect, Build Rapport, Exchange, Tie up Transaction,

Nurture for the future

ABOUT THE AUTHOR

Bruce Lawson has over 30 years' experience in training, coaching, sales and development. He is a Master practitioner of NLP, a registered Hypnotherapist with GHC, a qualified practitioner of EFT, an advanced trainer in EMO and holds a diploma in stress, trauma and PTSD. He is the creator of the COPE® system of development. Bruce has sold and trained in the UK and abroad and has coached and run courses at all levels from CEO down.

Bruce is also the creator of *FCO²*, *the ultimate formula for a happy life* – his first book available through Amazon.

This book, G.R.O.W.T.H.S. U.P.®, is available as an e-book and in hard copy though Amazon. It is supported by video blogs, a Facebook page a website and Twitter. Look out for upcoming workshops given both in person and via Skype.

- For more information email Bruce at: growthsup@gmail.com
- See his website: www.growthsup.co.uk.
- or Facebook page: www.facebook.com/copewellbeingsgrowthsup
- or follow him on Twitter @copewellbeing

BACK COVER

Do you hate sales and selling yet need to increase revenue and customer numbers?

Are you the owner, manager or entrepreneur of a small to medium size business who loves the business itself but hates having to sell it?

Are you a senior manager of a larger company who needs their managers and staff to also generate more revenue and customers; and know how difficult it is to get them motivated to sell?

If this rings a bell and looks right, then this book is for you!

G.R.O.W.T.H.S. U.P.® stands for: Generating Revenue Without The Hassle of Sales whilst Uplifting Performance. In this book you will find a natural method to increase the number of your customers and improve your revenue generation without the stress and upset that a normal "Sales process!" engenders.

This book and its accompanying project is a natural method to help increase customer numbers and improve revenue generation without the stress and upset that old fashioned, manipulative, scripted, sales processes cause.

This book is for anyone that needs to ensure their G.R.O.W.T.H.S. U.P.® but hates the idea of "Selling", "Closing", "Demanding money" or manipulating others.

The book contains a set of tools to help you create an effective, relaxed, natural, conversation that will lead to revenue enhancement and more customers. It then applies those tools, on a customer journey, that takes you from sourcing the potential customer to converting them to a lifelong supporter and purchaser of your goods and services. All in natural, relaxed and stress free method. G.R.O.W.T.H.S. U.P.®'s combination of tools and applications works.

To enhance your potential for growth this book is supported by a website, video blog tips and coaching workshops available in person or via skype. For more details see contact information inside.

www.ingramcontent.com/pod-product-compliance
Lightning Source LLC
Chambersburg PA
CBHW051900170526
45168CB00001B/184
* 9 7 8 1 5 1 4 3 3 2 4 7 4 *